D0391955

A Guide to
Strategic Thinking

A Guide to Strategic Thinking

Building Your Planning Foundation

George L. Morrisey

Jossey-Bass Publishers • San Francisco

Copyright © 1996 by George L. Morrisey and Jossey-Bass Inc.,
Publishers, 350 Sansome Street, San Francisco, California 94104.
Copyright under International, Pan American, and Universal
Copyright Conventions. All rights reserved. No part of this book may
be reproduced in any form—except for brief quotation (not to exceed
1,000 words) in a review or professional work—without permission in
writing from the publisher.

Substantial discounts on bulk quantities of Jossey-Bass books are
available to corporations, professional associations, and other
organizations. For details and discount information, contact the
special sales department at Jossey-Bass Inc., Publishers.
(415) 433-1740; Fax (800) 605-2665.

For sales outside the United States, please contact your local
Simon & Schuster International Office.

Manufactured in the United States of America.

Library of Congress Cataloging-in-Publication Data

Morrisey, George L.
    Morrisey on planning : a guide to strategic thinking : building your
planning foundation / George L. Morrisey.
        p.   cm. — (The Jossey-Bass business and management series)
    Includes bibliographical references and index.
    ISBN 0-7879-0168-7
    1. Strategic planning.   2. Creative ability in business.
I. Title.   II. Series.
HD30.28.M6537   1996
658.4'012—dc20   95-34924
                                                                              CIP

FIRST EDITION
HB Printing   10   9   8   7   6   5   4   3   2   1

THE JOSSEY-BASS BUSINESS AND MANAGEMENT SERIES

THE
MORRISEY ON PLANNING
SERIES

A Guide to Strategic Thinking
Building Your Planning Foundation

A Guide to Long-Range Planning
Creating Your Strategic Journey

A Guide to Tactical Planning
Producing Your Short-Term Results

Contents

CHAPTER THREE

But First, What Are Your Strategic Values?   21

CHAPTER FOUR

Who Are You and How Will You Function? (Part One)
Developing Your Organization's Mission   35

CHAPTER EIGHT

What Happens Next?
Building a Bridge to the Rest of
Your Planning Process 99

Introduction to the Series

My experience in working with the planning process over a period of many years with a wide variety of client organizations has led me to the conclusion that there are three phases managers must go through in this process, each characterized by a distinctly different mind-set. The first phase is *strategic thinking*, which focuses on the more *intuitive* aspects of the process leading to the development of the organization's mission, vision, and strategy. This phase is designed to create the organization's future *perspective* while establishing a foundation from which all major planning decisions will be made.

The second phase is *long-range planning*, which calls for a combination of intuitive and *analytical* thinking leading to projections of future *positions* the organization wishes to attain. This phase is designed to validate and activate the mission, vision, and strategy created during the first phase.

The third phase is *tactical planning*, which is primarily an analytical approach with some intuitive overtones that leads to specific actions affecting the organization's current *performance*. This phase is designed to produce the short-term results needed to carry out the organization's mission and to reach the future positions that have been projected.

I have established this three-book series to reflect how several of my clients have chosen to work through the planning process. By design, the books are

- Short, practical, and how-to oriented. They are a length that is more comfortable for most managers than many of the longer, more theoretical books on the subject.

- Easily portable and appropriate for introspective reading during quiet times (such as on an airplane trip).

- Designed as an interrelated series, yet each book stands on its own as a guide to doing a more effective job on the aspect of planning addressed in that particular book.

- Useful source materials for seminars and workshops on planning; they also may be used as pre-reading and advance assignments for facilitated planning events and as ongoing reference books for individual managers and management teams as they work with the process on the job.

The first book, *A Guide to Strategic Thinking: Building Your Planning Foundation*, will help you get your planning team started by determining your organization's principles and values as well as the strategic direction in which you should be moving. While there is heavier emphasis in this book on the roles of the CEO and the senior management team, it provides guidance for all managers throughout your organization who must contribute to the strategic planning process.

The second book, *A Guide to Long-Range Planning: Creating Your Strategic Journey*, provides the tools for establishing a focus on the positions toward which your organization needs to strive in such areas as future markets, future products and services, technology, human competencies, and financial projections. It will be useful for all managers in your organization who need to focus on the future.

The third book, *A Guide to Tactical Planning: Producing Your Short-Term Results*, will provide all managers (executives, middle managers, first-line supervisors, and individual contributors alike) with a methodology for achieving meaningful short-term results on both a planned and an ad hoc basis.

The brief nature of each book makes this series a resource that participating managers can easily use on an ongoing basis as well as in preparing for formal planning efforts. While the emphasis in each use will be different, all managers have a vested interest in making both the strategic and tactical planning processes work in their areas of responsibility. All of the books contain examples drawn from individual departments and work units as well as from the perspective of the total organization. Some of these examples are identified as coming from specific organizations with which I have worked. Others represent adaptations from the efforts of organizations I have chosen not to identify. All of the examples are real.

As with any set of tools, the effective use of these books is dependent upon the desire and skill of the person using them. They are not designed as a substitute for sound managerial judgment. Rather, they are intended to enhance that judgment in order to help you and other managers in your organization do a more consistent and creative job of planning to meet future as well as current needs. Best wishes in your journey!

Acknowledgments

I have been privileged to be associated with many of the top management thinkers of our time. They have significantly influenced my work, as resources and in many cases as direct collaborators. They include, of course, my two previous coauthors of Jossey-Bass publications—*The Executive Guide to Strategic Planning* and *The Executive Guide to Operational Planning*—Patrick Below and Betty Acomb, as well as Bonnie Abney, Louis Allen, N. H. Atthreya, Joe Batten, Arthur Beck, Fred Clark, Donn Coffee, Tom Connellan, Peter Drucker, Marie Kane, Alec Mackenzie, Bob Mager, Dale McConkey, Henry Migliore, Howard Mold, George Odiorne, Gene Seyna, Brian Tracy, and Glenn Varney.

I am especially appreciative of the many fine managers within the organizations I have served as a consultant, who have allowed me the opportunity to validate the concepts and techniques of effective planning while providing me with excellent feedback that helped immeasurably in refinement of the process. I would like particularly to acknowledge two outstanding managers who have demonstrated how this process can work effectively over a long period of time in a variety of increasingly responsible positions:

Chris Ellefson of BHP Minerals International and Nelson Marchioli of Burger King.

I have been blessed to be associated for several years with a group of professional speakers, trainers, and consultants that we, its members, refer to as our mentor group. These colleagues have encouraged, critiqued, and otherwise helped me to hone my ideas and to properly position my publications as well as my services to clients. They are Tom Callister, Lola Gillebaard, Jane Holcomb, Eileen McDargh, Jack Mixner, and Karen Wilson.

Finally, but far from least, I will be eternally grateful for the continuous support I receive from my business partner, my best friend, and my loving wife for many years, Carol Morrisey.

Merritt Island, Florida   G.L.M.
April 1995

Preface

Portions of the present book were adapted from some of my earlier books on Management by Objectives and Results (MOR) as well as a more recent book I coauthored with Patrick J. Below and Betty L. Acomb, *The Executive Guide to Strategic Planning* (1987). The latter book included both *strategic thinking* and *long-range planning*. However, as I indicated in the introduction to this series, my experience since that time in assisting many client organizations with the planning process has prompted me to address strategic thinking and long-range planning in two separate books because of the distinct differences in both developing and implementing these two planning processes. I have also made several modifications in the strategic thinking process as first introduced in *The Executive Guide to Strategic Planning*. The present book reflects the way I am currently assisting clients in making the strategic thinking process work for them.

The first substantive change is the introduction of the identification of *strategic values* as the first step in preparing your planning foundation. While I do not recommend a separate statement of strategic values, such values permeate all strategic thinking decisions. They represent the philosophical convictions of the managers who are charged with guiding your organization on a successful journey.

The next major change was introducing *vision* as potentially separate from *mission*. While I still believe unequivocally that the creation of your organization's mission statement is the single most important document you will produce in your entire planning process, I have come to realize the potential benefit of having a separate brief and inspiring vision statement of what you believe the future should look like for your organization in the eyes of your customers, employees, owners, and other important stakeholders. Simply stated, your mission describes the concept of your organization, the nature of the business in which you are involved, why you exist, who you serve, and the principles and values under which you intend to function; your vision expresses your dream of the future. I have also included a chapter on developing unit roles and missions, since many organizations are recognizing the need to involve all segments in the strategic planning process.

In the earlier book on strategic planning, *strategic analysis* was included under strategic thinking, between mission and strategy. I have used this step more in the long-range planning part of the process, so I have modified it significantly and incorporated it into the second book in this series.

Strategy continues to focus on the future direction of the organization. I offer two options in addressing strategy. The first option is use of the *driving force* approach first introduced in Ben Tregoe and John Zimmerman's book *Top Management Strategy* (1980). This valuable approach still serves many organizations, although I have introduced several variations in looking at strategic factors. I refer to the second option as the *questioning* approach, which is most useful when you do not anticipate any significant controversy around strategic factors such as those described in the driving force approach.

A Guide to Strategic Planning focuses largely on the intuitive part of the planning process, encouraging managers to reach agreement on the fundamental concept and direction of the organization before determining specific future positions to pursue.

How Can This Book Be Used?

There are several ways you can use this book, including as a

- Guide for management teams at both the total organization level and the unit level who wish to reach agreement on their values, mission, vision, and strategy as a foundation for their planning efforts.

- Guide for individual managers and management teams in their ongoing strategic thinking and planning efforts.
- Text for an in-house workshop on strategic planning skills for managers.
- Text for a college or university extension program or a public seminar on strategic planning. (Note: the content and examples are directed primarily toward participants who wish to apply it in their own work areas, not toward those studying management theory.)
- Reference guide for internal and external consultants charged with helping organizations with their planning efforts.
- Individual study guide for the working manager.

For self-study, I recommend the following approach:

1. Read the Preface and Chapters One, Two, and Eight for an overview of the planning philosophy and process being presented.
2. Determine which of the following alternatives best serves your individual needs:

   a. Selective learning of specific techniques to supplement your existing knowledge
   b. Concentrating on learning how to develop and use a mission statement for the total organization or for your specific unit
   c. Learning and applying the entire process to your organization or unit

3. If you have selected 2(a) as most appropriate for you, the recommendation is easy. Study and practice those steps that will satisfy your needs.
4. If 2(b) seems best for you at the moment, Chapters Four

and Five will be of most value to you. It's important to become familiar with both chapters as you determine how to approach the development of your own mission statement.

5.   If you are ready to commit yourself to 2(c), I recommend starting with reaching agreement among the members of your management team on what strategic values are most important. With that as a foundation, you can proceed more easily with determining your mission, vision, and strategy.

6.   Use the book as a continual reference as you continue your application of the strategic thinking and planning process.

7.   Don't get discouraged when you hit the inevitable periods of setback and frustration in your strategic planning efforts. Stay with it, and both your satisfaction and effectiveness will increase as you continue to develop your skill.

Get ready now to become an even more effective manager than you already are as you explore the intuitive side of strategic planning!

Merritt Island, Florida   G.L.M.
August 1995

The Author

George L. Morrisey is chairman of The Morrisey Group, a management consulting firm based in Merritt Island, Florida. He received his B.S. (1951) and M.Ed. (1952) from Springfield College. He has more than twenty years of experience as a practicing manager and key specialist with such organizations as the YMCA, First Western Bank, Rockwell International, McDonnell Douglas, and the U.S. Postal Service, as well as more than twenty years as a full-time consultant, professional speaker, and seminar leader. He has personally assisted more than two hundred business, industrial, service, governmental, and not-for-profit organizations throughout the world in the areas of strategic and tactical planning.

Morrisey is the author or coauthor of fifteen books prior to this series, including *Management by Objectives and Results in the Public Sector* (1976); *Management by Objectives and Results for Business and Industry* (1977); *Getting Your Act Together: Goal Setting for Fun, Health and Profit* (1980); *Performance Appraisals for Business and Industry* (1983); *Performance Appraisals in the Public Sector* (1983); *The Executive Guide to Operational Planning* (with Patrick J. Below and Betty L. Acomb, 1987); *The Executive Guide to Strategic Planning* (with Patrick J. Below and Betty L. Acomb, 1987); *Effective Business and Technical Presentations* (with Thomas L. Sechrest, 1987); and *Creating Your Future: Personal Strategic Planning for Professionals* (1992). He is the author and producer of several learning programs on audiocassette and videocassette, all directed toward helping individuals and organizations become more effective and self-fulfilled.

A professional's professional, Morrisey received the Certified Speaking Professional (CSP) designation in 1983 and was recognized in 1984 with the CPAE (Council of Peers Award for Excellence), the highest recognition granted to a professional speaker by the National Speakers Association. In addition, in 1994, Morrisey was the sixteenth recipient of the annual Cavett Award, named in honor of the founder of the National Speakers Association, Cavett Robert. Morrisey is a former member of the boards of directors of the Association for Management Excellence (originally the International MBO Institute) and the National Speakers Association.

For further information on Morrisey's services, please contact:

The Morrisey Group
P.O. Box 541296
Merritt Island, FL 32954-1296
(800) 535-8202, (407) 452-7414, Fax (407) 452-2129

A Guide to Strategic Thinking

CHAPTER ONE

What's This All About?

A Foundation for Your Strategic Planning

If you don't know where you are going, any road will take you there.
This is a truism attributed to the Koran, and one that often applies
to the situations in which we find ourselves as managers. Who are
we? Why do we exist? Where are we going? These are fundamental questions that we as managers need to ask periodically to make
certain that we and the organizations for which we are responsible
keep our efforts properly focused. In fact, *focus* is probably the single
most important word in the planning dictionary. One of the most
significant reasons for having a plan in the first place is to avoid
spinning our wheels on efforts that make little or no contribution
to our reasons for existence.

One of the sometimes justifiable criticisms of the planning
process is that it tends to be more analytical than intuitive. In
reality, both intuition and analysis are essential to effective planning. The process can be visualized as a continuum between these
two extremes, as shown in Figure 1.1. Your position on the continuum may vary radically depending on where you are in the
planning process. One of the reasons for dividing this treatment
of the planning process into three separate books is to describe
and emphasize the significance of these variations in thought
processes. Simply stated, the *strategic thinking* portion of the
process relies heavily on intuition, with only a modest amount of
analysis; the *long-range planning* portion requires a balance
between the two; and the *tactical planning* portion relies heavily
on analysis, with intuition serving primarily as a check and
balance.

Intuitive ——————————————————————————— Analytical
Strategic Thinking   *Long-Range Planning*   *Tactical Planning*

Figure 1.1 The Planning Continuum

One way of looking at these three major components is to relate them to the "three P's of planning": *perspective, position,* and *performance*. The emphasis of each of the components could be described as follows:

Strategic thinking leads to *perspective*

Long-range planning leads to *position*

Tactical planning leads to *performance*

Naturally, the relationships are not as clear-cut as shown here. However, drawing this distinction is a good way to begin this discussion. One thing we have to recognize is that planning is a *human* process far more than a system. We should be far less concerned about getting conformity to a set of rules and regulations than about getting people's minds focused on the direction in which they should be moving. At the same time, we must remain flexible both in terms of what our final destinations should be and in terms of what we need to do to get there.

The three components and their elements are shown in Figure 1.2. Note how each of the first two components penetrates the next one, leading ultimately to effective plan implementation.

What Is Strategic Thinking and Why Is It Important?

Individual strategic thinking involves the application of experience-based judgment to determine future directions. Organizational strategic thinking is the coordination of creative minds into a com-

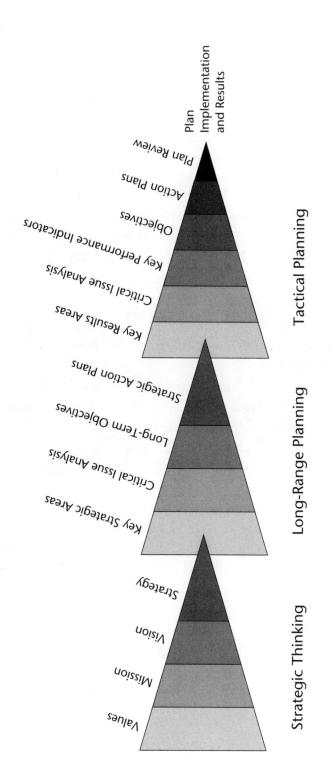

Figure 1.2 The Planning Process

mon *perspective* that enables your organization to proceed into the future in a manner fulfilling to all concerned. The purpose of strategic thinking is to help you exploit the many challenges, both predictable and unpredictable, in your future, rather than prepare for a single probable tomorrow. Strategic thinking is important because

- Sound judgment, even though frequently based on inadequate information, is the single most important thing any organization expects of its managers.
- To be effective, collective judgment depends on your organization's key decision makers having a clear and consistent vision of what the future direction of your organization should be.
- Your organization's vision is based more on how your key decision makers see and feel than on the results of any systematic analysis.
- Strategic thinking incorporates values, mission, vision, and strategy, which tend to be intuitive (feeling-based) rather than analytical (data-based) elements.
- Reaching agreement on these elements among members of your management team is an essential prerequisite to effective planning.

Strategic thinking forms the foundation for strategic decision making. Without this foundation, subsequent decisions and actions are likely to be fragmented and inconsistent with the long-range health of your organization.

What Is Long-Range Planning and Why Is It Important?

Building on the agreements that result from your strategic thinking, you and your management team will be better able to address critical issues that will impact the carrying out of your organization's mission and strategy. Long-range planning involves the application of both intuition and analysis to determining future *positions* your organization needs to attain. Traditionally, long-range planning has frequently been an extrapolation of history, projecting future results based on current and past experience. In today's rapidly changing world, such practice could be a blueprint for disaster. Long-range planning must be seen as a dynamic process that is flexible enough to allow and even to encourage modification of plans to respond to changing circumstances. Long-range planning charts your journey to future success. It is important because it

- Keeps you focused on the future as well as the present
- Reinforces the principles espoused in your mission, vision, and strategy
- Encourages cross-functional planning and communication
- Builds a bridge to your short-term tactical planning process (where you will *implement* your long-range plan)
- Encourages managers to look at planning from a macro perspective
- Saves time, reduces conflict, and increases the power of human endeavor

Long-range planning is a process that brings your management team together to translate your mission, vision, and strategy into tangible future results.

What Is Tactical Planning and Why Is It Important?

Tactical planning is the ongoing involvement of managers and key employees in producing plans for your total organization as well as for their individual units. Its purpose is to ensure that organizational *performance* in the production of short-term results is consistent with the strategic direction of your organization and makes the most effective use of its available resources. It is important because it

- Translates strategic thinking and long-range planning into specific measurable results
- Emphasizes team planning that gives participants ownership in the plan and its projected results
- Provides a means for carrying out short-term plans and for ensuring understanding and commitment to them
- Is different from both strategic thinking and long-range planning in that it is largely analytical, with heavy emphasis on data-based decision making
- Is more internally focused as well as more specific and detailed than strategic thinking and long-range planning
- Typically has a one-year horizon although it supports future direction
- Can be used as an ongoing process for addressing problems or opportunities, as well as for establishing annual plans
- Is a vital source of information before budget preparation
- Can be used effectively by individual contributors as well as by work units, departments, divisions, and your entire organization.

Tactical planning is the process that helps you pursue worthwhile opportunities, improve your results, avoid or minimize your losses, and provide continuous feedback so you can take corrective action when needed.

What's Involved in the Strategic Thinking Process?

As pointed out earlier, strategic thinking is much more of an intuitive or feeling process than either long-range or tactical planning.

Initially, it is more important to have congruence among your management team members on the nature and scope of your business, the principles under which you intend to operate, and the direction in which you should be moving as an organization than it is to be concerned about how you will achieve the results you may need. Strategic thinking is the arena for dreaming about the future without being hampered by practicalities. In other words, not only is it acceptable to project what you would like your organization to become without being particularly concerned about whether or not it can be done, it is also desirable.

For starters, let me define how I will be using the terms *values, mission, vision,* and *strategy*:

1. *Values* represent the philosophical convictions of the managers who are charged with guiding your organization on a successful journey. Some of these values will be fixed, such as your positions on ethics, quality, and safety. Other values, such as responsiveness to customers, product/service diversity, and profitability, may vary over time, depending on the nature of your business. They serve as a foundation for your thinking as you approach mission, vision, and strategy.

2. *Mission* is a statement describing the concept of your organization, the nature of the business in which you are involved, why you exist, who you serve, and the principles and values under which you intend to function.

3. *Vision* is a representation of what you believe the future should look like for your organization in the eyes of your customers, employees, owners, and other important stakeholders. The vision statement may be separate or it may be included as a part of your mission statement.

4. *Strategy* addresses the direction in which your organization should be headed, its *driving force*, and other major factors that will help you determine your future products, services, and markets.

In my view, a maximum of three separate statements will flow out of the strategic thinking process: the mission statement, the vision statement, and the strategy statement. You may reach the conclusion that these three can be combined into two or even one. I have seen organizations with as many as five separate statements, which in my judgment frequently tends to confuse more than clarify the position of the organization. There is a benefit, however, to looking at values, mission, vision, and strategy separately at first to see what insight each provides. Then you can decide whether it is more advantageous to combine some or all of them or to keep them separate. At the very least, you will want to have a statement of *mission*, which in my judgment is the single most important document you will create in your planning process.

Where Does Strategic Thinking Fit with Other Current Approaches?

There has been virtually an epidemic of new concepts introduced in recent years that have strategic implications. Some of these concepts provide significant additional contributions to management theory and practice, while others are primarily warmed over versions of existing ideas with new labels.

One of the problems I see with a concept that has a catchy label is that the label itself limits its lifespan. I know, because I rode the crest of one of the more popular concepts of recent years: MBO—Management By Objectives—or what I called MOR—Management by Objectives and Results. MBO was a very popular approach to planning for nearly twenty years (longer than many other "labels"), until it too fell into disrepute. This was due more to poor or inappropriate implementation than to any problems with the process itself. Many organizations today are operating successfully using MBO/MOR as their approach to planning, with or without using the specific label.

There is an old adage that says *a tool is only as good as the person who uses it.* A precision screwdriver can be used to open a can of beer, but I would not recommend that use of such a tool. Management tools are no different from other skill-demanding tools. They require training in their use, and effective and consistent *follow-through* if they are to achieve the anticipated benefits.

With a few notable exceptions, nearly every new management concept that is introduced will produce worthwhile benefits if it is used in the prescribed manner. Each concept can also have unsatisfactory or even disastrous consequences if it is not used properly. Unfortunately, many concepts end up being the *management program du jour.* My observation is that calling something a "program" almost dooms it to failure from the outset, because many managers view a program as something that has to be done *in addition to their jobs.* Generally, a concept is truly effective when managers practice it *without referring to the label.*

Let's take the *quality* movement as a case in point. Who can argue with the importance of operating a business in a quality manner? The emphasis in recent years on *TQM* (*Total Quality Management*) and its many variations has had a beneficial effect on developing *quality awareness* within organizations. Quality is one of the values I will be addressing in Chapter Three. Yet, I question whether quality can best be served through the institution of a specific program. For example, I received a call a few years ago from an executive in a well-known company indicating that the company was hoping to win the Malcolm Baldridge Award within the next two years and asking if I could help them put together a planning program that would lead to that. I politely declined, suggesting that I would be more comfortable helping them implement a planning process that would make the management of their company more effective, which conceivably might eventually lead to such recognition. I indicated to them, however, that trying to win the award was the wrong motivation, one that would send inappropriate signals to people within the company and elsewhere. They did not retain my services.

Many excellent management concepts have been introduced in recent years, such as *TQM, reengineering, benchmarking,* and *competitive resourcing,* to mention a few. Each has some excellent ideas, tools, and techniques that can help improve your management practices. (I comment on several publications related to these in the Annotated Resources section of this book.) As a practicing manager, you owe it to yourself and to your organization to remain current on what is happening in the world of management theory and practice. However, at the risk of belaboring the obvious, you should never be looking for something new to try out just because it is the latest rage. Rather, you should study such materials in order to improve on what you are already doing well, in addition to identifying ways to address concerns that are not receiving the kind of attention they deserve. *Management is and always will be more of an art than a science.* So, put on your artist's smock and get to work creating your latest masterpiece.

In Summary

- Strategic thinking provides the foundation for strategic planning and is largely intuitive in nature.
- Strategic thinking leads to perspective, while long-range planning leads to position and tactical planning leads to performance.
- Strategic thinking addresses values, the philosophical convictions of the managers charged with guiding your organization on a successful journey; mission, the overall concept of your organization; vision, what your organization should look like in the future; and strategy, the direction in which your organization should be headed.

The next chapter will focus on the people who need to be involved in your strategic thinking process and how they should approach their related responsibilities.

CHAPTER TWO

Who Are Your Strategic Thinkers and How Should They Function?

There was a time when strategic planning, particularly the *strategic thinking* aspects of it, was considered to be almost exclusively the province of top management. (I used to believe that myself.) It has become increasingly evident in recent years, however, that every organization needs the active involvement of all its key decision makers if it is to be successful. This is essential both to get valuable input from those on the firing line and, perhaps more important, to ensure their ownership of and commitment to the final product. While the formal strategic thinking process usually starts with the chief executive officer (CEO) and the senior management team, it must permeate the rest of the organization fairly quickly if it is to be effective. My focus in this chapter is on the various roles each level of management must play in the strategic thinking process, with particular emphasis on senior management and on when and how to get others involved. I will expand on the various aspects of the process in subsequent chapters.

What Is the Unit President Concept?

The Unit President concept has proven very useful in pinpointing responsibility for planning. Whether you are CEO of your organization, a division or department head, a middle manager, a first-line supervisor, or an individual contributor within a larger unit, consider yourself president of your own company. Consider everyone within the company with whom you must relate, including your boss, as your board of directors. The responsibility of a president is to clearly identify a direction for the organization that will satisfy the board and deliver the results that will meet the board's needs. As Unit President, you need to make certain that your unit is headed in a direction that is at least compatible with your entire organization. Once that direction is clear, you will generally have a great deal of freedom in the way you manage your "company" as long as you produce the desired results. This principle and the rest of the concepts in this book are applicable whether you function as a manager in private enterprise, government, or a not-for-profit organization. (While the Unit President concept will have more application in *tactical planning*, it's important to keep it in mind throughout the entire planning process.)

Who Does What in Strategic Thinking?

The ultimate responsibility for the development and implementation of the *total* organization's strategic and tactical plans lies with your CEO (or whoever is designated as your organization's key decision maker) and the senior management team, which includes major department heads, one or two key staff advisers, and whoever will be guiding your planning process. If you are a member of the senior team, you are responsible for seeing that the process cascades down through all of the levels under your leadership and for getting employees to generate ideas upward for possible inclusion in your organization's plan. This cascading process is desirable whether you are focusing on *strategic thinking, long-range planning,* or *tactical planning.* Let's begin by looking specifically at the roles of the key players in the *strategic thinking* process.

• *Your* CEO must demonstrate strong leadership if the strategic thinking process is to receive proper attention throughout your organization. This leadership includes being actively involved in the development process from the outset and allocating sufficient personal time for completion of assignments. Since strategic thinking will lead to identification of your organization's values, mission, vision, and strategy (in separate or combined form), the results of these efforts must be ones your CEO can clearly and enthusiastically support. Your CEO may at times be required to take a strong position to ensure that decisions are made and that the process does not become bogged down when it appears that consensus cannot be reached.

- *Senior management team members* function in dual roles. If you are a member of this team, you need to recognize that you serve as an extension of the office of the CEO. In theory, your CEO could complete the process independently, but most executives recognize that they cannot do it alone, and the merging of divergent ideas will usually provide a stronger and more useful outcome. It needs to be clearly understood, however, that when you are working in this arena, you are representing the interests of the entire organization, not primarily those of your own functional or program responsibilities. Your second role, as indicated earlier, is to provide leadership in getting input from and communicating to others within your areas of responsibility.

- Members of your *board of directors* may be actively involved in the entire strategic thinking process, or they may function primarily in a review and approval mode, depending on the board's size and structure and the interest level of its members. Board members of not-for-profit organizations, such as trade and professional associations, educational institutions, or community service agencies, frequently will be actively involved in the development process either as a total body (if the board is of a manageable size) or, more frequently, through a strategic planning committee (possibly the executive committee) that will do the initial development, with a review by the entire board. Most corporate boards, however, will look to the CEO and the senior team for leadership in the initial development of the concept and direction of the organization.

- The *planning coordinator* is someone within the organization who is designated as responsible for making sure that the entire planning process comes together. A member of the senior team, sometimes the CEO, typically assumes this role. The planning coordinator needs to be someone with good administrative skills who wants the responsibility. Whoever performs this role usually does so throughout the planning process to ensure continuity and may perform any or all of the following duties:

Establishing and monitoring the planning schedule

Coordinating and handling logistics of planning meetings

Documenting and distributing meeting records

• The *planning process facilitator's* responsibilities may be carried out by an internal or external coach/facilitator, preferably someone who does not have a strong personal vested interest in the outcome. Although a member of the senior team may have the skill to perform this role, he or she should not do so because senior team members need to be free to take advocacy positions on certain issues and to express personal convictions during discussions. To be effective, your facilitator must remain neutral while guiding the discussion.

Your planning process facilitator needs to have both the respect of participating executives and personal confidence because it may be necessary at times to confront individual members of the team. An internal consultant brings in-depth knowledge of the organization and generally is more accessible than an external consultant. An external consultant brings a broader and more diverse experience and is usually perceived as more neutral than an internal consultant. An effective internal/external consulting team brings the best of both worlds.

Your planning facilitator may perform any or all of the following duties:

Designing or modifying the planning process

Training/coaching managers involved in the planning process

Designing and facilitating planning meetings

CEO coaching/counseling

• Other managers, by adopting the Unit President concept, are responsible for the development of appropriate strategic thinking documents for their own units. Naturally, if such a process has been started by higher-level management, you will need to be certain that what comes out of your process is supportive of that of the total organization. If such a process has *not* been started at higher levels, you may still proceed with it at your level, using your best judgment to ensure that what comes out of your unit's efforts is at least compatible with where the rest of the organization appears to be headed.

How Much Time Is Required?

The amount of time required to complete the strategic thinking part of the planning process will vary substantially depending on the size and complexity of your organization, the nature of your business, and whether you are starting from scratch or building on what has already taken place. My experience in working with a wide variety of organizations is that you can reasonably expect to come up with draft statements covering your mission, vision, and strategy in a two-day off-site meeting *provided* that all members of your planning team have done their homework. My general recommendation, however, is to combine the strategic thinking phase with your *long-range planning* process and schedule a series of two or three two-day meetings thirty to sixty days apart. The information and insights generated by the strategic thinking portion will be extremely helpful as you proceed with the identification of your key strategic areas, analysis of your critical issues, determination of your long-term objectives, and establishment of your strategic action plans. Furthermore, by scheduling a series of meetings, with specific assignments in between, you will have an opportunity to get feedback on your initial efforts and make appropriate modifications as you proceed. You also need to recognize that each participating manager will have to invest several hours of individual preparation time to make the meetings as productive as possible.

One thing to bear in mind if you are approaching this formally for the first time is that *you do not have to come up with a complete strategic plan in your initial effort.* That ambition could prove either overwhelming or superficial. You might wish to concentrate on clarifying your strategic values and developing an initial draft of your mission statement, with the expectation that you can modify these and move on to other aspects of the strategic planning process at a later time. In other words, use an incremental approach that will ensure you are making progress—much like a football team concentrating on making a series of first downs rather than going for a touchdown on every play.

How Do We Get Other Important Stakeholders Involved?

One of the real strengths of this process is the opportunity to involve others who have a vested interest in the outcome of your strategic thinking efforts before, during, and after your initial development efforts. These "others" could include employees who may not be actively participating in the development process, customers, outside representatives, suppliers, strategic alliance partners, community representatives, and perhaps even some of your competitors, if cooperative efforts could benefit all concerned. (This does not mean violating any antitrust restrictions, of course.)

Before

At the very least, you may wish to inform selected stakeholders that you are proceeding with the development or modification of your mission, vision, and strategy and invite them to share their thoughts informally. While many will not respond to such an invitation, at least they will be aware of what you are doing, and curiosity, if nothing else, is likely to keep them interested.

Other approaches to getting stakeholders involved include:

- Developing a brief series of questions, similar to those described in subsequent chapters, to be distributed to selected stakeholders for comment and returned prior to your initial meetings
- Conducting a series of focus group meetings designed to get their input on such questions
- Appointing a task force with a cross-section of interested parties who can help highlight factors that need to be addressed

During

If you are scheduling a series of meetings, it may be appropriate for members of your planning team to meet with other people from their own units and perhaps from other units to get some interim feedback on the progress you are making. This is especially important as you complete your initial draft statements, to make certain that your words convey the meaning you intend. (Subsequent chapters contain examples of the kinds of questions you may wish to ask.)

After

Once your planning team has agreed on the appropriate statements to provide the kind of guidance that will support future decision making, it's important that you communicate these statements to those who will be most affected. In so doing, you may wish to point out that these statements are still subject to modification based on feedback received. Here are several ways in which you can communicate this information:

- Publish your mission, vision, and strategy statements, collectively or separately, together with any interpretation you may feel is necessary. (If you have done a thorough job in your development process, there should be little or no need for interpretation.)

- Meet with representatives of various stakeholder groups (probably starting with employees) either individually or in small groups and discuss the implications of the results of your efforts for them individually and collectively as well as for the entire organization. My recommendation is that you circulate the materials either in advance of or during the meeting and *ask participants to interpret the meaning of the documents* rather than interpreting the documents for them. By doing so, you have a better chance of getting candid feedback on the clarity of your message.

- Circulate draft documents of these materials together with a series of feedback questions for people to react to. (See the end of Chapter Four for examples of such questions related to mission interpretation.) This method is especially useful in highly decentralized organizations or ones in which it would be difficult or too time-consuming to bring groups of people together for this purpose. As a facilitator, I have used this approach with organizations in which a small group developed the initial drafts and a larger group met later to refine the statements and proceed to the next steps in long-range or tactical planning. By having their replies returned to me as the facilitator, I was able to identify specific concerns or trends that needed to be addressed in subsequent meetings.

- Circulate the draft statements with a cover letter indicating that they will be reviewed and possibly modified at a designated future time, such as in six months, for example.

The principal to keep in mind is that these materials need to be perceived as *living documents* that will be used to guide ongoing decision making. They are not academic recordings to be filed and forgotten or ignored when it is convenient to do so. You can be sure that some of your stakeholders will challenge you when it is clear that your actions are not in line with positions taken in your strategic thinking efforts.

Can Strategic Thinking Be Used for Team Building?

Absolutely! My observation is that the sharing and interaction that takes place in a facilitated strategic thinking effort can be one of the most powerful processes available for developing a sense of unity and mutual support among members of your management team, whether at the executive or unit level. My admittedly biased point of view suggests that there is greater team development value in having your team members go through this kind of exchange than there is in many of the purely interpersonal team development efforts that some of my consultant colleagues advocate.

In Summary

- Strategic thinking needs the active involvement of all your organization's key decision makers in various stages.
- The Unit President concept (you are president of your own "company" regardless of your position in your organization) is a useful way to pinpoint responsibility for planning.
- The ultimate responsibility for the development and implementation of your organization's strategic and tactical plans lies with your CEO and the senior management team.
- A planning process facilitator who does not have a strong personal vested interest in the outcome will help make your planning efforts more productive and objective.
- Strategic thinking will require a modest investment of time and effort by your key decision makers.
- Other important stakeholders, who may not be a direct part of your formal strategic thinking efforts, need to be involved before, during, and/or after your formal efforts in order to ensure their support as you proceed.

- Strategic thinking can be one of the most powerful processes for developing a sense of unity and mutual support among members of your management team.

We can now proceed to the assessment of your strategic values as a precursor to developing your mission, creating your vision, and formulating your strategy.

CHAPTER THREE

But First, What Are Your Strategic Values?

Although my focus in this book is on creating and using your mission, vision, and strategy, it is important that you and other members of your management team first assess and agree on what your organization's strategic values are or should be, before developing your perspective on the future. Every organization develops its own personality, which is a reflection of the personal values and convictions of the managers who are charged with guiding the organization on a successful journey.

Why Is Agreement on Our Strategic Values Important?

There is so much that needs to be done to make your organization successful that you cannot afford to spend a lot of your time and energy working at cross-purposes with the other members of your management team. For example, suppose one member of the team viewed your employees strictly as a disposable resource; another saw them as the heart and soul of your organization, whose total welfare was to be maintained at all costs; and your position were somewhere in between. (Please note that I am not evaluating any of these positions as "good" or "bad.") Can you picture some of the conflicts that are likely to arise when you must make decisions that will impact both the financial health of the organization and its productive direction? What might be even more disconcerting, of course, would be if people with such polarized positions did not acknowledge them openly, yet managed their areas of responsibility with that particular focus. I am not suggesting that there will not or should not be conflict among members of your management team regarding the relative importance of certain values. After all, managed conflict can lead to productive growth. I am suggesting, however, that such conflicting views need to be out in the open and there has to be a clear understanding among your team members about which values are fixed and which ones may be reasonably modified. Having a clear and open agreement on your strategic values will help you

- Determine the breadth and scope of your organization's efforts
- Establish what types of business you should or should not be in
- Both establish your expectations and communicate them to others
- Recruit the kind of people who will work effectively within your organization
- Determine how you will conduct your business
- Establish meaningful priorities

What Are Some Specific Strategic Values?

There are an almost infinite number of factors that you might consider to be strategic values. I recommend that you concentrate on no more than eight to ten values and that they be ones that will have a *major* impact on the future of your organization. Some values may be "givens" and may not need to be listed at all. Other values will remain fixed as long as you are in business, but may need to be kept visible. Still others may vary from time to time depending on where you are in your business cycle. I will introduce you to a checklist shortly that will help you make these choices.

The following paragraphs discuss several values that various organizations have found useful, but you need to develop a list that will be most meaningful for you.

- *Ethics.* This may be one of those values that is a "given." I would like to think that any reader of this book will operate in an ethical manner in business, almost without thinking about it. Calling attention to ethical concerns may only raise questions in others' minds. For example, what is your reaction when someone says, "To be perfectly honest with you . . ."? Does it cause you to wonder whether there are times when that person may be less than "perfectly honest"? Conversely, if you happen to be operating in a business environment in which the ethics of some practitioners may be in question (telephone solicitation is one such business that comes to mind), specifically articulating that you value ethical behavior may help set your organization apart.

- *Quality.* Like ethics, this also may be a "given" for you. If you do choose to identify it specifically as a value, you may need to define what you mean and, of course, you will need to make certain that you back up your position with appropriate action.

- *Safety.* If you are in an industry like chemical manufacturing, mining, or transportation, safety had better be at or near the top of your list of values. If yours is an industry in which accidents are rare, you will need to maintain safety awareness, but it is not likely to be a strategic value.

- *Environment.* Like safety, this value will be extremely important for industries that have a major impact on the environment either through their products or processes, but it may be of minor concern to other industries unless members of management wish to take a proactive stance on environmental issues.

- *Innovation, the cutting edge.* If you choose this as one of your strategic values, please recognize that both cost and risk are associated with it. Being on the cutting edge implies that you will be ahead of your competition and that you are willing to experiment with new ideas that may not be fully tested. Keeping up with the technology in your field is essential to your organization's success, but that in itself does not represent innovation.

- *Image in your industry.* Is it important for your organization to be readily identified as one of the leaders in your industry or is it preferable to remain relatively obscure except in relation to those with whom you do business? Either position might be appropriate for you, but it needs to be clear to all concerned. It will certainly impact some of your future actions.

• *Image in your community.* This value is similar to image in your industry but it is designed to reach a much wider audience. Part of this value may be related to your maintaining a specific public image for marketing purposes, or it may reflect your views on corporate citizenship and community leadership. Once again, your position here will impact some of your future actions.

• *Fun.* More and more organizations are finding it beneficial for their places of business to be seen by customers, employees, or preferably both, as fun places to be. How does this fit with your business?

• *Responsiveness to customers.* Your position here might range from acceptance to total commitment. At one extreme, customers (defined as individuals, not organizations) will be served only by designated employees at a pace that will not interfere with ongoing employee responsibilities. At the other extreme, any employee will be expected to stop whatever they may be doing to take care of a customer's concerns. The nature of your business and your own perspective on the importance of responsiveness in relation to that business will help you determine how this value should be focused. Although total commitment to serving customers may be the hallmark of certain retail operations, it may not be practical or even desirable in a clinic or an engineering firm.

• *Human resources.* As suggested earlier, this value could range from treating employees as disposable at one extreme to attending to their total well-being at the other. One extreme is inhumane and may backfire (as major-league baseball discovered in the 1960s); the other may be cost-prohibitive.

• *Profitability.* It's a "given" that making a profit is essential to the survival of any business. Even so-called not-for-profit organizations need to generate more income than they project in expenses or they will not be around for long. If this becomes one of your strategic values, however, you need to determine whether you will limit your ventures only to those that produce high financial return or if you will engage in some efforts that will show only marginal or even negative return. If there will be a mix between the two, what is an acceptable level? (I will address the issue of return/profit more directly in Chapter Seven when we explore strategy.)

• *Strategic alliances.* Such alliances provide an opportunity to partner with other independent organizations that have complementary or supplementary capabilities. They are another way of addressing expansion needs that has become increasingly popular in recent years. The strategic alliance is considerably more than a typical vendor or supplier relationship. It implies mutual commitments based on equal or proportional ownership of the outcomes. These alliances may be temporary, to focus on a particular major project, or they may have a sense of permanence, if ongoing mutual benefits are perceived. Does this option present a real synergistic value for your organization, or do you prefer to remain largely self-contained? Is there a balance between the two extremes that makes sense for you?

• *Product/service diversity.* Here you might wish to focus on a single class of product or service, such as the sale of specialty items or providing travel assistance, or you may wish to be open to any product or service that you could produce or provide. There are many examples of organizations that have been successful at both extremes as well as in between. Should you be looking for new product or service opportunities or should you stay with what you know best?

• *Market/customer diversity.* At one extreme, this value would represent niche marketing to a particular industry, such as real estate, or a particular ethnic group. At the other extreme, your company would welcome opportunities to serve anyone.

• *Standard/customized products.* Do you wish to focus exclusively on "off-the-shelf" products or services, or are you more interested in customizing products or services to meet individual needs and wants? Is there an appropriate balance between these two options?

• *Expansion.* What is your position on expansion? Do you prefer to stay largely at your current size and in your current structure (in which case expansion would not be a strategic value), or are you anticipating a very rapid expansion over the next several years? If you are thinking about expanding your business, offering new products or services, building more capability, or upgrading your staff, are you more inclined to develop these options internally or to acquire the capabilities from outside sources? Developing options internally generally will take longer and may be more costly in operating funds than acquiring them. Acquisition, on the other hand, usually can be achieved more quickly and may require significant capital funding, but could result in some control, quality, or morale problems. In reality, no organization is likely to function exclusively at either extreme. If this is one of your values, you need to determine whether your primary emphasis will be on *development* with *acquisition* as your backup, or the other way around.

• *Organizational structure.* Do you value having a *decentralized* organizational structure, in which each operating unit functions independently with a bare minimum of central services and control? Or does a more *centralized* structure with most major decisions being made at the upper levels of the organization make more sense? Is there a point between these two extremes that will work more effectively for you? Is your position on this issue important enough to establish it as a strategic value?

• *Geographic concentration.* Either because of personal preferences or for legitimate business reasons, do you wish to be located in a particular part of the country or world? Is your geographic focus primarily local, state/regional, national, hemispheric, or global? To what extent will this focus influence your future actions?

As indicated earlier, this is not an exhaustive list of potential strategic values, by a long shot. You need to be highly selective in the ones you choose as major influencers, and you need to include others that may be important to you that have not been covered here. Figure 3.1 is a checklist that incorporates all the strategic values I have described. Additional lines are provided for you to add other values that you need to consider as well.

How Do We Assess Our Strategic Values?

I recommend that for best results you distribute copies of this checklist (permission to copy is hereby granted) or one that you have made up yourself to all members of your management team with instructions to complete it on their own, without discussing it with others, and to bring it with them to a team meeting where the discussion of values is an agenda item. If you have a designated facilitator for the meeting who is not a member of the team, you may wish to have copies returned to him or her for compilation in advance of the meeting. By having team members complete the checklist ahead of time, those who may prefer a more thoughtful and less spontaneous response will have an opportunity to express themselves more fully. Figure 3.2 is an example of a completed checklist.

The instructions to participants for completing the checklist are as follows:

1. Review the descriptions in this chapter and check off those listed strategic values that you believe are appropriate for your organization. Feel free to reword any that are not clear to you or that might be more useful in your organization if worded differently.

2. In addition to those listed, add any strategic values that you believe should be considered.

3. For each value you have checked, circle the point between the two extremes that you consider appropriate.

4. Enter any comments you feel are appropriate to support your position.

Figure 3.1 Assessment of Strategic Values

                                              Comments

Ethics
not important • • • • • most important _____

Quality
not important • • • • • most important _____

Safety
not important • • • • • most important _____

Environment
not important • • • • • most important _____

Innovation, the cutting edge
not important • • • • • most important _____

Image in your industry
not important • • • • • most important _____

Image in your community
not important • • • • • most important _____

Fun
not important • • • • • most important _____

Responsiveness to customers
not important • • • • • most important _____

Human resources
not important • • • • • most important _____

Profitability
not important • • • • • most important _____

Strategic alliances
not important • • • • • most important _____

Product/service diversity
narrow range • • • • • wide range _____

Market/customer diversity
narrow range • • • • • wide range _____

Standard/customized products
standard • • • • • customized _____

Expansion
develop within • • • • • acquire _____

Organizational structure
centralized • • • • • decentralized _____

Geographic concentration
local   regional   national   hemispheric   global _____

Others

Copyright © 1995 by Jossey-Bass Publishers, San Francisco. From *Morrisey on Planning: A Guide to Strategic Thinking,* by George L. Morrisey. Permission to reproduce is hereby granted.

Figure 3.2 Assessment of Strategic Values (example)

Comments

Ethics
not important   •   •   •   •   •   most important   This is a "given" for us

✓ *Quality*
not important   •   •   •   •   ⊙   most important   We must be seen as a top quality organization

Safety
not important   •   •   •   •   •   most important   Not a significant factor

Environment
not important   •   •   •   •   •   most important

✓ *Innovation, the cutting edge*
not important   •   •   ⊙   •   •   most important   We need to be alert to innovation but can't afford high risk ventures

✓ *Image in your industry*
not important   •   •   •   ⊙   •   most important   We have a good image that needs to be sustained

Image in your community
not important   •   •   •   •   •   most important

✓ *Fun*
not important   •   •   •   ⊙   •   most important   We need to work harder to make this a fun place to work

✓ *Responsiveness to customer*
not important   •   •   •   •   ⊙   most important   Our customers are our life blood

✓ *Human resources*
not important   •   •   •   •   ⊙   most important   We need to invest more in helping our people to grow

✓ *Profitability*
not important   •   •   ⊙   •   •   most important   Profitability is essential for our growth, but not our primary focus

Strategic alliances
not important   •   •   •   •   •   most important   Worth revisiting next year

Product/service diversity
narrow range   •   •   •   •   •   wide range   OK

Market/customer diversity
narrow range   •   •   •   •   •   wide range   OK

Standard/customized products
standard   •   •   •   •   •   customized   OK

✓ *Expansion*
develop within   •   •   •   ⊙   •   acquire   Growth will come largely through acquisitions

Organizational structure
centralized   •   •   •   •   •   decentralized

✓ *Geographic concentration*
local   regional   national   hemispheric   ⟨global⟩   Heavy emphasis needed on foreign expansion to sustain our growth

Others

5. If requested, make a copy of your completed checklist and send it to your facilitator in advance of the meeting.

6. Bring your completed checklist with you to the meeting and be prepared to share your point of view on what your organization's stated strategic values should be.

Following are the instructions for the meeting facilitator:

1. If appropriate and practical, receive copies of completed checklists in advance of the meeting and make a brief compilation of responses. You may discover that you can eliminate some of the listed values that no one has checked off.

2. At the meeting, you may wish to post a tally of the number of advance responses to each of the listed values as well as a list of any additional ones that have been identified. Or you may prefer to take a tally from the group during the session itself. Invite a limited discussion of the implications of the total tally before getting into discussion of any specific identified value.

3. Invite discussion of each of the values checked, even if only one person checked it (that individual may have an important perspective that others may have overlooked). Encourage open discussion of conflicting points of view. If possible, reach a consensus on which of these values deserve to be considered for your final list.

4. For those values making the cut, try to reach a consensus on each value's position between the two extremes. Be sure to allow sufficient time for differing points of view to be aired.

5. Reach a consensus on no more than eight to ten strategic values (less might be even better) that will guide your strategic thinking throughout the rest of the process.

6. Whether or not you choose to publish the resulting list of strategic values, each value should be stated in a brief phrase

or sentence that establishes your organization's position on that value. This may be done by the total group in session, by a group of two or three from the group, or by an individual, to be presented for final review and agreement at a subsequent session.

Here are a few examples of value statements:

- Safety comes first, production will follow.
- Quality is Job One!
- We will not knowingly produce a product or engage in a practice that will negatively affect the world in which we live and work.
- Fun and productivity go hand in hand.
- Our people are our greatest asset.
- We will be world-class in customer satisfaction.
- The prime purpose of profit is to help build our business.
- We will actively pursue market opportunities where we have, or can attain, dominance.

How Should We Use This List of Strategic Values?

The most important use of this list will be as a ready reference as you develop your organization's mission, vision, and strategy. Some or possibly all of your identified values will be stated directly or indirectly in your mission statement. By going through your values assessment before developing your mission, you will be able to give your mission statement the proper values emphasis. (I'll cover the development of your mission statement more thoroughly in the next chapter.)

Your vision statement, which normally is developed after your mission statement, is likely to be almost entirely values-based. Its purpose is to provide an inspirational and motivational picture of where you are headed as an organization. Likewise, your values will play a significant role in defining your driving force and placing your strategic priorities into place as you develop your strategy or strategic direction.

Normally, I recommend against publishing your list of values since they will be addressed in your mission, vision, and strategy statements, and a statement of values is just one more document, which might dilute the effect of your message. However, you may find it desirable to publish your list for limited distribution to important stakeholders such as customers, employees, and owners, if your mission, vision, and strategy don't provide the proper emphasis. Just be careful about oversaturation with relatively esoteric material. Also, be certain that every one of your stated values clearly reflects the way you function on a day-to-day basis or you will destroy your credibility.

Your list of strategic values will also be a worthwhile reference as you proceed with developing your long-range and tactical plans, as well as for ongoing decision making.

In Summary

- Reaching agreement on your strategic values is an important foundation step to determining your mission, vision, and strategy.

- Some of your values will remain fixed as long as you are in business, while others may vary from time to time depending on where you are in your business cycle.

- You should concentrate on no more than eight to ten strategic values that will have a major impact on the future of your organization.

- Some or possibly all of your identified values will be stated directly or indirectly in your mission statement and will be addressed when you create your vision and determine your strategy.

Now that you have assessed your strategic values, you can proceed with the development of your mission statement, which in my judgment is the single most important document to come from your planning process.

CHAPTER FOUR

Who Are You and How Will You Function? (Part One)

Developing Your Organization's Mission

I believe unequivocally that the creation of your organization's mission statement is the single most important step you can take in the entire planning process. An effective mission statement will serve as a foundation for all major decisions that you and your management team will ever make. According to my definition, a *mission* statement differs from a *vision* statement in that it is more comprehensive, encompassing the following major elements:

- The concept of your organization
- The nature of your business
- The reason your organization exists
- The people you serve
- The principles and values under which you intend to operate

A vision statement, which will be described in more detail in Chapter Six, is a brief (one or two sentences) philosophical representation of how you want to be seen by your customers, employees, owners, and other important stakeholders. In my previous writings, I incorporated vision as a part of a mission statement. My position now, based on more recent work I have done with organizations, is that the two are related but serve different purposes. A vision statement is designed to inspire and motivate those with a vested interest in the organization's future. A mission statement is designed to provide firm guidance in making important management decisions. In many cases, your vision will be a brief adaptation of a portion of your mission statement.

In this chapter I will focus on the creation and use of a mission statement for the entire organization. In Chapter Five I will show how to adapt the process for use in individual units within the total organization such as divisions, departments, or branches.

Why Do We Need a Mission Statement?

You will find that having a succinct but comprehensive statement will help you to

- Establish and maintain consistency and clarity of purpose throughout your organization
- Provide a frame of reference for all major planning decisions to be made by you and your management team as well as by other units within your organization
- Gain commitment from everyone within your organization through clear communication of the nature and concept of your organization's business
- Gain understanding and support from those people outside your organization who are important to your success

The principal application of the mission statement is as an internal guide for all major decision makers within your organization, so that any plans that are developed can be tested for compatibility with your total organization's mission. Without a clear statement of purpose for your entire organization, it's easy for resources to become diffused and for individual units to operate completely independently, often at cross purposes. In other words, your mission statement should be a visible document that can enable virtually everyone within your organization to focus their efforts in a manner that is supportive of your organization's overall purpose.

Externally, your organization's mission statement will provide clear communication to such groups as major customers, suppliers, and the financial community, as well as your board of directors, your stockholders, and/or your parent organization. While its primary purpose is not to function as a public relations document, the mission statement can serve effectively in that manner if it has been properly prepared, although your vision statement may be more useful in that respect.

Who Is Involved in the Development of Our Mission Statement?

As was described in Chapter Two, the primary responsibility for developing a mission statement for your entire organization lies with your CEO (or whatever title your organization's chief decision maker carries) and members of the senior management team. Secondary responsibility lies with other key managers throughout the organization who need to review the initial draft and raise questions or offer suggestions on how the statement can be made more effective and useful. (I will describe a process for doing so later in this chapter.)

So, let me reemphasize a position I took in Chapter Two, that the role of members of the senior management team in developing a mission statement is as an extension of the office of the CEO. As such, they need to function from the perspective of the total organization, regardless of the impact of decisions on their own particular units or areas of responsibility.

Since a mission statement is conceptual, broad-based, and comprehensive, members of your planning team need to do some independent study and thinking about what should go into your mission statement *before* coming together as a group to discuss and create that statement. Here are some suggestions for doing this:

- Read or skim this entire book with emphasis on Chapters One through Four.

- Review other books, articles, and written materials that are particularly relevant to the future of your industry, your organization, and the markets or customers you expect to be serving in the future.

- Review mission statements and other documents related to future direction that may have been created by a parent organization or peer organizations with whom you must interact. *Caution:* your mission statement should not be a carbon copy of such statements but it will need to be compatible with them.

- You may also wish to review mission statements from other organizations in your industry or related industries for ideas, but not as an alternative to doing your own creative thinking. (The American Management Association, The Conference Board, and other such organizations have files of mission statements available to members for review.)

- Write your answers to the questions that will be discussed in the next section, or a modified version of them. This exercise serves two purposes. The first is to ensure that all participants will be giving constructive thought to these concerns prior to getting together as a group. The second is to provide an opportunity for those participants who may prefer to study and reflect on such questions to participate in your meeting on an equal basis with those who tend to be more spontaneous in their responses.

- Complete the Assessment of Strategic Values (Figure 3.1) described in Chapter Three, either individually or as a total group. It's important that your team members reach some agreement on your organization's values either in advance of your mission development session or as a preliminary step in such a session.

What Are the Questions We Should Address?

Here are some generic questions and some discussion of their implications that will help you identify factors that need to be included in your mission statement. Although you will not necessarily include answers to all of these questions in your statement, responding to them requires strategic thinking, and your answers will be useful in other parts of your strategic planning process even if they are not included in your mission statement. You may wish to modify these questions or include some additional ones to make them more relevant for your particular organization. The worksheet that is included at the end of this chapter as Figure 4.1 contains the questions discussed here. Note that the first question has four subparts designed to examine all aspects of both your present and future business.

1a. *What business(es) are we in?* Your starting point must be to articulate where your efforts are being focused now. You may respond that your organization is a single major business such as retail sales, financial services, or manufacturing. If appropriate, you may wish to be more specific about the nature of your business—for example, retail clothing sales, banking, or furniture manufacturing. If you are in two or more major businesses that are clearly separate from each other even though related, they should be identified as well—for example, retail clothing sales for men, women, and children; commercial banking, personal banking, and trust services; or furniture manufacturing for the home and office. A particular service, such as tailoring and alterations, would not be considered as a separate business if it exists strictly to support one or more of the other businesses and would not stand alone as it is currently structured.

1b. *What businesses could we be in?* Drawing on the capabilities and resources you currently have or might acquire, what are some businesses that are at least worth exploring for future expansion? A clothier might be looking at footwear, jewelry, and cosmetics, for example. A bank could explore investment, escrow, and tax services. A furniture manufacturer might consider cabinets, carpeting, and interior decorating services. Let your mind run free as you explore possibilities, as long as there is a reasonable rationale for considering such businesses. (It probably wouldn't make much sense for a clothier to look into offering tax services.)

1c.   *What business(es) should we be in?* This is where reality needs to take over. It may be that continuing and possibly expanding your current business for the foreseeable future makes the most sense for you. There may be ample opportunity for the kind of growth you want. Conversely, there may be a declining market for your current business and you may need to expand into other areas in order to survive or at least to sustain the kind of growth that is appropriate for you. One way to start is by looking at the industry in which you are, or should be, represented, and then at your organization's particular niche within that industry. You could also specify what your organization has been charged to accomplish, both financially and in terms of service to the marketplace, by your board of directors, parent company, or other higher-level body.

1d.   *What business(es) should we not be in?* This is another reality check. Could some of the businesses you are considering present major risks that could adversely affect your core business? Would the investment you would have to make, in time and expertise as well as money, be more than the probable return you might receive? A clothier who is considering adding a jewelry business had better take a hard look at the downside of such a venture before signing a long-term contract with a supplier.

2.   *Why do we exist (what is our basic purpose)?* Although many organizations perceive profit or financial return as their reason for existence, it is rarely, if ever, their sole reason. What are some of the purposes, in addition to the financial ones, to which your organization should aspire? These may be service to a particular customer base, service to humanity, contribution to technology, recognition for achievement, and provision of a creative outlet for your founders and/or employees, to mention a few.

3.   *What is unique or distinctive about our organization?* Every organization, if it is to continue to be successful, needs to have one or more characteristics that set it apart from other organizations engaged in a similar business. You need to determine what this is for your organization, for marketing purposes as well as for giving direction and focus to your organization's efforts.

4. *Who are or should be our principal customers, clients, or users?* Many organizations have a series of customers whose needs have to be satisfied before their products or services reach the ultimate user. A manufacturer of consumer goods, for example, usually has to depend on a retail outlet (their direct customer) to get products to the eventual purchasers (their ultimate users). A hospital normally can serve a patient (their ultimate user) only if a doctor (their direct customer) places the patient in that hospital. Although there are exceptions, most manufacturers of computer peripherals recognize that their principal customers are the original equipment manufacturers (OEMs), through whose efforts their products eventually reach the end users. You need to identify both types of customers, when applicable, in order to properly define your business focus.

I have used alternative words—*customers, clients, users;* you can select whatever term is appropriate to your business. It's important, however, that you keep the concept of *customer* in front of you, regardless of the business in which you are engaged. A customer is someone whose needs and wants you are in business to satisfy. In responding to this question, you need to address customers rather than *markets* in order to clearly identify the tangible recipients of your services. Getting a clear picture of who your customers are and the order in which their needs and wants must be satisfied is a critical step in determining how your business should be projected.

5. *What are or should be our principal market segments, present and future?* Next, you need to identify markets (where your customers function) in broad categories, not in the detail you might expect from a market analysis. These segments can be defined in terms of such categories as geographic type (local, regional, national, global), type of industry (automotive, hospitality, real estate), size and type of businesses in your target markets (small, medium, large, family-owned, public or private corporations, governmental or not-for-profit organizations), occupational focus (engineering, health, sales), age (children, young marrieds, retirees), and economic/social status (middle income, unemployed, ethnic, college graduates).

6. *What are or should be our principal products/services, present and future?* Identify here the primary deliverables that your customers, clients, or users expect to receive from you. You should think in terms of groups of products or services, such as major appliances, accounting services, or business insurance, rather than individual items. You may wish to identify certain supporting services, such as customer training or maintenance, if they are revenue producing or if they represent a substantial amount of resource allocation. Put your emphasis on mainstream products and services, not on the products and services you might make available on an occasional basis in response to individual customer requests (unless, of course, customized products or services are "mainstream" in your business). What additional major products or services should you consider offering in the future?

7. *What are or should be our principal outlets or distribution channels, present and future?* How do you reach the end user? Is it through direct sales, marketing representatives, brokers or agents, independent distributors, direct mail, telemarketing, home shopping networks, centralized or decentralized storage, and/or retail outlets (your own or others)? Are there outlets or channels that are worth considering for the future that you may not be using now?

8. *How is our business different from what it was three to five years ago?* What major changes have taken place in your industry, the marketplaces you serve, the economy, the environment? What is different now about the technology you use, your competition, your organizational structure, financing, labor mix, and product/service mix? What major issues are still unresolved?

9. *What is likely to be different about our business three to five years in the future?* You need to identify those things that are inevitable, such as demographic or technological changes, and those that you can make happen and should give serious attention to, such as your position in the marketplace or your production capability. Some of the factors identified in question 8 may need to be revisited in terms of their future implications. Here is your oppor-

tunity to do some "blue sky" thinking, generating ideas that may or may not be valid but that at least ought to be examined. These ideas can also serve as a starting point for some brainstorming that may be appropriate during your planning meeting.

10. *What are or should be our principal economic concerns, and how are they measured?* Every organization, to survive and be successful, has certain specific economic concerns that must be satisfied. If you are a profit-making organization, your mission statement should include a commitment to profitability and/or growth. You need to have a clear and common understanding among your team members as to how you will measure profit. Will it be return on assets/equity/invested capital, percent of sales, gross margin, or some other financial indicators? Will you look at growth in terms of sales, revenue, capacity, or diversity? Will you measure it in absolute amounts or as a rate of growth? If your organization is in the public sector or operates as a not-for-profit organization, you may wish to consider a concept such as cost-effective use of available resources or increased service at no or low increase in relative cost.

11. *What philosophical issues, values, and priorities are or should be important to our organization's future?* The completion of your strategic values assessment will be especially helpful here. Identify those values that need to be specifically articulated in your mission statement and convert them into clear statements of major belief that will directly affect the way your organization will conduct its business. For example, if the leaders in your organization have strong concerns about the environment, you may wish to state that "we will not knowingly introduce any product or process that has a destructive impact on the world in which we live." Are there any factors not specifically identified in your values, such as productivity or management approach, that should be considered as you prepare your mission statement?

12. *What special considerations do we have in regard to the following stakeholders (as applicable)?*

- Owners/stockholders/investors/constituents
- Board of directors
- Parent organization
- Legislative/regulatory bodies
- Employees
- Customers/clients/users
- Strategic alliance partners
- Suppliers
- Communities in which we function
- General public
- Others (specify)

The purpose of this question is to make certain that in responding to the first eleven questions you have not overlooked any significant factors that impact specific groups of people with a vested interest in your organization's future. If there are any particular items you need to address either in your mission statement or at some other point in your strategic planning process, you should identify them here so they can become a part of related discussions.

How Do We Prepare Our Mission Statement?

A method that I have found works extremely well for starting the development of a mission statement, or for reviewing and revising an existing one, is to schedule an off-site planning meeting for that purpose. It is virtually impossible to do this work at the organization's offices. There are too many distractions. A hotel conference room, a conference center, or a resort are frequently used for this purpose. The effective development of your mission statement requires the full and undivided attention of the members of your management team. Anything less than that is likely to produce a less meaningful and useful statement. (An optimum size group for such an effort is six to ten people, although I have facilitated groups as large as sixteen. There need to be enough people to provide effective interaction, yet the size of the group should be limited to keep the process from getting bogged down. Larger groups typically require more time to complete the process.)

Each member of the team needs to complete the worksheet provided in Figure 4.1, "Clarifying Your Organization's Mission," or a customized version of it, prior to the planning meeting, following the instructions provided. The worksheet is designed to get your team members to look at the big picture of the total organization rather than concentrating on their own areas of responsibility. The explanations in the previous section may help. As noted earlier, you will not include all of the answers to these questions in your mission statement. However, discussion of them is a significant early step in strategic thinking and your answers will impact later parts of the planning process. I believe it is critical for participants to write down their answers to the questions in advance of the meeting as a form of crystallizing their own thinking.

If the team has not already reached agreement on the organization's strategic values, I recommend doing so at your planning meeting before going through the mission development process. Articulation of these values will provide some important perspectives that will assist in the process and also will help develop a climate for open discussion.

I cannot overstress the importance of having a skilled facilitator for your mission development process, someone who does not have a strong personal vested interest in the outcome. Although some of your team members may have excellent facilitative skills, they need to be free to take advocacy positions on issues on which they have strong convictions. (While my bias suggests that a professional consultant who specializes in planning facilitation is most useful in this role, retired executives, executives from other organizations, college or university faculty, or trade association staff may also function effectively in this role.) Your facilitator needs to remain neutral on the issues while drawing out differing points of view. It's up to your facilitator to make sure that innovative thinking takes place, that no individual dominates the discussion, and that the group reaches a consensus on the key factors to be included in your mission statement. (*Consensus*, in this case, means reaching agreement on a statement that is at least *acceptable* to all participants.)

The process starts with your facilitator asking participants to read their answers to questions 1a and 1b, one person at a time. These responses are posted for all to see. (I prefer a flipchart, but other media, such as computer-generated visuals, overhead transparencies, chalkboard, whiteboard, and so forth, are also useful for this purpose.) Responses that are similar to those already posted may be recorded with an additional check mark. The only questions or comments permitted during this posting are related to clarification of meaning, not to the validity of the statements. Once all answers to these questions have been posted, the meeting is opened for discussion of differing points of view. Some consolidation of answers is likely to occur during this discussion.

Next, participants are asked to give their responses to 1c and 1d. They may choose to modify their written responses based on discussion that took place related to the previous questions. The discussion that follows these second two questions should lead to the highlighting of certain words or phrases that need to appear somewhere in the mission statement. This same process will continue for each of the succeeding questions, although the facilitator may determine at some point that going to each participant individually may no longer be necessary and that open responses will be just as productive and less time-consuming. (An alternative to this approach, if time is limited and if significant controversy does not appear likely, is to have the worksheets turned in to the facilitator, who will summarize and post the various answers before the meeting. Please recognize, however, that this will significantly reduce the open discussion that is one of the strengths of this process.)

When all questions have been answered, your team needs to review all responses and reach agreement on which words or phrases need to be included in the initial draft of the mission statement. Unless the group is relatively small (six or seven participants at the most), I recommend that the facilitator meet with two or three team members to draft an initial statement for review and refinement by the entire team later in the meeting or at a subsequent meeting.

A mission statement developed by following this process is typically one-half to one page in length. It normally includes an umbrella statement (fifteen to thirty words) that identifies the conceptual nature of your business, both now and in the foreseeable future, and your reason for existence. Following that, you may wish to use a statement that begins "In support of this mission, we are committed to" followed by a series of bulleted statements (typically four to six) of specific philosophy and overall operation similar to those shown in the examples in the next section. Remember, however, that these sample statements were appropriate for the organizations that created them and will not necessarily be appropriate for yours.

You need to devote a minimum of a half day to this effort, with the potential of a full day if there is a wide diversity of opinions on the part of team members. You should allow whatever time is necessary to reach consensus. Shortchanging this step will seriously impair the rest of your planning process.

A word of caution: don't include anything in your statement of mission that you are not willing to back up with action. If any portion of your mission statement is perceived as not really reflecting the way you do business, it will destroy the credibility of your planning efforts. This is why you need to have additional discussion among your team members before releasing your draft statement for review by others.

When your team is in general agreement with the draft statement, I recommend that you circulate it among some of your stakeholders: board members, parent organization executives, selected (or all) employees, selected customers, and others whose perspective you value. The following questions may prove useful in getting useful feedback. (A sample worksheet for this purpose is included as Figure 4.2 at the end of the chapter.) If practical, you may wish to meet with individuals or small groups to discuss their responses. At the very least, you need to express appreciation for their responses and provide feedback about how they are being used.

- Which words or phrases in our draft mission statement are not clear or meaningful to you? Please explain if possible.
- Which items in our draft mission statement are we addressing effectively now?
- Which items are we *not* addressing effectively now?
- What is missing that should be included?
- What is included that should be modified or eliminated?
- What other comments or suggestions do you have for making our mission statement a more meaningful and useful document?

What Are Some Examples of Organizations' Mission Statements?

Here are some mission statements developed by specific organizations in a wide variety of businesses (which are used here with permission). The terms used in each are especially appropriate to these organizations and would not necessarily be applicable to other, similar entities.

American Red Ball Worldwide Movers

The mission of American Red Ball is to provide quality, cost-effective relocation services for businesses, government agencies, and individuals throughout the world. This will be accomplished through a unified company approach based on a fair return for owners, agents, drivers, and employees. In support of this, we are mutually committed to

- Providing active and involved leadership in a changing world, leadership that is responsive to the needs of our customers and business partners
- Assisting agents, drivers, and employees in their business and professional growth and recognizing them for their accomplishments
- Being proactive in identifying changing customer needs, wants, and expectations that create business opportunities
- Making safety an overriding obligation in all our operations
- Achieving managed growth through prudent reinvestment of company profits

Atwood Mobile Products

The mission of Atwood Mobile Products is to design, develop, manufacture, and market products and services for recreation and specialty vehicles and associated niche markets on a global basis. We operate with the highest levels of integrity while providing a rewarding quality of life and a fair return for our customers, employees, owners, suppliers, and communities. In support of this, we commit to the following:

- To develop and maintain partnerships with our customers and suppliers, leading to high-quality, superior-value products and services that are responsive to consumer needs
- To provide an environment that promotes and rewards the development and involvement of all employees
- To actively pursue market opportunities where we have or can attain dominance
- To be a visionary, innovative, and creative organization, leading to growth and continuous improvement
- To actively contribute to the industries we serve and the communities in which we live

Auspex Systems

Auspex Systems provides products and services that deliver high throughput, accessibility, and integrity for customers' data within the general computing industry. Our purpose is to provide innovative products in a timely manner that meet or exceed customers' needs while providing a fair return to investors and employees, and to have fun while doing it. We are committed to

- Always treating our customers, our suppliers, and our associates as we wish to be treated
- Being world-class in customer satisfaction and quality, and recognized as such by the industry (customers, suppliers, employees, and competitors)
- Being a great place to work, as viewed by our employees, by providing an open and supportive environment
- Empowering all employees to take ownership for continuous improvement
- Being the leading supplier of data servers in the high end of the client workstation market and a competitive supplier of data servers in the general purpose computing market

The Prudential California Realty

It is the mission of The Prudential California Realty to provide exemplary real estate sales and related services that are based on the highest possible levels of trust and integrity. In maintaining this standard of excellence, the company is dedicated to sustaining a professional environment that promotes the success of our clients, associates, employees, and owners. Supporting this adherence to excellence, The Prudential California Realty is committed to

- Leading the industry in providing real estate services in select premier and complementary markets throughout California

- Providing superior leadership and management throughout the organization

- Recognizing performance and achievement at all levels and creating a professional environment that promotes personal fulfillment and career development for the company's associates, managers, and employees

- Providing innovative support services in response to associate and client needs

- Maintaining premier international services and marketing distribution networks that support local sales activities and promote a global presence for the firm

- Remaining the leading independently owned real estate firm in California

American Lung Association of Gulfcoast Florida

The mission of the American Lung Association of Gulfcoast Florida is the promotion of lung health and the ultimate conquest of lung disease through education, research, and advocacy. In support of this mission, the Board of Directors, Regional Councils, volunteers, and staff are committed to

- Developing and delivering innovative, quality programs through Regional Councils in response to assessment of community needs

- Increasing public awareness of the Association's role in promoting lung health and preventing lung disease

- Seeking and maintaining relationships in the community to enhance delivery of program services

- Advocating initiatives that promote lung health and air quality in both indoor and outdoor environments

- Developing innovative ways of increasing financial and other resources and prudently managing the use of those resources

- Assuring an atmosphere supportive of volunteer and staff recruitment, retention, and professional growth that promotes pride and cohesiveness in the organization

National Tour Association

The National Tour Association (NTA) is an organization of companies that plan and operate quality tours throughout North America. NTA's mission is to help improve the performance and profitability of its tour company members and to ensure value for Supplier and Destination Marketing Organization members' membership investment, with special emphasis on services that members cannot efficiently provide for themselves. In support of this, the association is committed to

- Continuing and maintaining the association's reputation for excellence and integrity
- Conveying to members the need to conduct their businesses and execute services to consumers in accordance with the highest standards of ethics and integrity
- Facilitating communication among all membership categories to provide a superior travel product
- Promoting travel in North America through the tour company members of NTA
- Representing members with regard to collective governmental and industry issues
- Developing research information and marketing assistance to enable members to remain competitive
- Providing education and membership benefits that meet or exceed those of comparable trade associations
- Exploring for members new business concepts and technology

Recreation Vehicle Industry Association

The mission of the Recreation Vehicle Industry Association (RVIA) is to be a high-quality national association representing, promoting, and protecting the interests of all recreation vehicle manufacturers, conversion vehicle manufacturers, and suppliers, with emphasis on facilitating the health and well-being of the industry, and providing services that members cannot provide as effectively or efficiently for themselves. In support of this, we are committed to innovative leadership in

- Promoting a positive environment that encourages the active involvement of members and staff and promotes unity and pride in the association
- Taking advantage of opportunities that benefit the industry
- Networking with organizations that have common interests
- Maintaining the financial strength of the association

In Summary

The development of a statement of mission for your organization is the first and perhaps the most important element in your planning process.

- It forms a foundation from which all other management decisions must be made.
- It requires careful thought and preparation on the part of your planning team, with ample time allowed for refinement of the various points of view that are likely to be expressed.
- It needs to be developed with the assistance of a skilled facilitator who does not have a vested interest in the outcome.
- It needs to be communicated to all important stakeholders, both for feedback on their interpretation and to help them relate more effectively to the business at hand.
- It needs to be reviewed annually, or whenever major changes take place, to be certain it is still relevant.

Once your organization's mission statement has been clearly established and approved, it should remain constant for an extended period. While it should be reviewed formally at least once a year, or any time a major change occurs in the nature of your business, it should not be changed unless it no longer provides the clear guidance you need for the future. In any case, I recommend that you go through the mission development process at least every three or four years *as though one did not exist.* Remember, in mission development, *the process is more important than the product.*

Chapter Five shows how this process can be modified and used in individual departments or work units. If that is not a major concern for you right now, you may wish to move directly to Chapter Six, which will show you how to create a strategic vision for your organization.

Figure 4.1 Worksheet for Clarifying Your Organization's Mission

1a. What business(es) are we in?
1b. What businesses could we be in?
1c. What business(es) should we be in?
1d. What business(es) should we not be in?
2. Why do we exist (what is our basic purpose)?
3. What is unique or distinctive about our organization?
4. Who are or should be our principal customers, clients, or users?
5. What are or should be our principal market segments, present and future?
6. What are or should be our principal products/services, present and future?
7. What are or should be our principal outlets or distribution channels, present and future?
8. How is our business different from what it was three to five years ago?
9. What is likely to be different about our business three to five years in the future?
10. What are or should be our principal economic concerns, and how are they measured?
11. What philosophical issues, values, and priorities are or should be important to our organization's future?
12. What special considerations do we have in regard to the following stakeholders (as applicable)?
    - Owners/stockholders/investors/constituents
    - Board of directors
    - Parent organization
    - Legislative/regulatory bodies
    - Employees
    - Customers/clients/users
    - Strategic alliance partners
    - Suppliers
    - Communities in which we function
    - General public
    - Others (specify)

Copyright © 1995 by Jossey-Bass Publishers, San Francisco. From *Morrisey on Planning: A Guide to Strategic Thinking*, by George L. Morrisey. Permission to reproduce is hereby granted.

Figure 4.2 Worksheet for Reviewing and Evaluating Your Draft
Mission Statement

(Place your double-spaced draft mission statement here.)

Worksheet

1. Which words or phrases in our draft mission statement are not clear
    or meaningful to you? Please explain if possible.
2. Which items in our draft mission statement are we addressing
    effectively now?
3. Which items are we *not* addressing effectively now?
4. What is missing that should be included?
5. What is included that should be modified or eliminated?
6. What other comments or suggestions do you have for making our
    mission statement a more meaningful and useful document?

Copyright © 1995 by Jossey-Bass Publishers, San Francisco. From *Morrisey on
Planning: A Guide to Strategic Thinking,* by George L. Morrisey. Permission to
reproduce is hereby granted.

CHAPTER FIVE

Who Are You and How Will You Function? (Part Two)

Developing Your Unit's Roles and Missions

As you prepare to develop a statement of roles and missions for your department or unit, many of the principles relevant to an organization's mission that were covered in Chapter Four will also be relevant here. There are, however, some distinct differences in approach to the statement of a specific unit. For example, I refer to the unit statement as a statement of roles and missions rather than of mission alone. This focus will help you to identify the variety of specific roles your unit may play or tasks it may perform in support of your total organization's mission, such as designing, testing, analyzing, manufacturing, or selling. It's not necessary, however, to separate roles and missions in your statement, because they overlap and are both part of your unit's commitments.

Also, each unit's statement must be clearly separate from other units' statements. No two units within a total organization should have identical roles and missions. If they do, the organization is inviting duplication of effort or, what may be worse, an effort gap. (Note: if your unit is in a distinctly separate business from that of the total organization, such as a credit card operation that is part of a financial institution, I recommend approaching mission development as though the unit were a separate company, following the process in Chapter Four.)

Why Should There Be a Statement of Roles and Missions for Each Separate Unit?

There are several reasons why each unit should have its own statement of roles and missions. Some of the more important factors are

- To ensure that all critical work is accomplished and that accountability is established for it, thus avoiding the problems that occur when everyone assumes that somebody else is doing it
- To reduce, if not eliminate, the likelihood of duplication of effort
- To ensure that individual employees within your unit clearly see the relationship between what they are doing and the apparent reasons for the existence of the total organization
- To ensure that effort is being expended on work that clearly contributes to, and does not detract from, the economic well-being of the total organization
- To reduce the likelihood of jurisdictional disputes among related organizational units
- To serve as a forum for resolution of misunderstandings or disputes within each unit as well as among related units

While a clear statement of roles and missions will not guarantee that these various factors will always be addressed appropriately, the absence of such a statement will inevitably lead to some of the negative consequences implied. In addition, of course, a valid statement of roles and missions is the baseline from which all your unit's objectives should be drawn. In other words, any objective you project (whether strategic or tactical) should be in direct support of your unit's statement of roles and missions; otherwise, serious questions should be raised as to whether any significant effort should be devoted to that objective at all.

Where Does My Unit's Statement of Roles and Missions Originate?

Ideally, a clear, concise, and comprehensive statement of mission for the total organization provides the basis for roles-and-missions statements of smaller units within it. However, if no organization-wide statement exists, you must create one, at least conceptually, before your unit's roles and missions can be defined. A similar definition may be required if your unit is part of a larger unit such as a division or department that does not have its own mission statement.

Figure 5.1 contains a series of questions for clarifying organizational unit roles and missions. They are similar to those for the total organization (Chapter Four) but are focused at the unit level.

Figure 5.1 Worksheet for Clarifying Unit Roles and Missions

1. What business is the total organization in? Why does it exist?
2. What business is my unit in?
3. Why does my unit exist (what is our basic purpose)?
4. Who are my unit's principal customers/clients/users? Are we primarily a production or support operation?
5. What are my unit's principal products/services/functions?
6. How do these products/services/functions contribute to the total organization's mission?
7. What is unique or distinctive about my unit's work compared to that of other units in the organization?
8. How is my unit's work different from what it was three to five years ago?
9. What is likely to be different about my unit's work three to five years in the future?
10. What should be my unit's economic commitment to the total organization?
11. What philosophical issues, values, and priorities are important to my unit's future (related to organization and/or department image, customers, employees, safety, environment, innovation/risk taking, administrative practices, and so on)?
12. What special considerations do we have (if not addressed above) in regard to
    - Upper management?
    - Customers/clients/users?
    - Employees?
    - Suppliers?
    - Peer organizations?
    - General public?
    - Others (specify)?

Copyright © 1995 by Jossey-Bass Publishers, San Francisco. From *Morrisey on Planning: A Guide to Strategic Thinking*, by George L. Morrisey. Permission to reproduce is hereby granted.

How Should Unit Statements Be Prepared?

I recommend the following step-by-step process as a logical method by which your unit's statement of roles and missions can be defined. Whether or not you follow each step precisely is a matter of choice and dependent on your circumstances.

1. Identify the total organization's mission (either from its formal statement or by your own assessment).
2. Identify the roles and missions of the major department or functional unit of which you are a part.
3. Determine appropriate answers to the questions posed in Figure 5.1 that are relevant for you. (When practical, involve your key employees in this discussion and analysis.)
4. Prepare a rough draft of your roles-and-missions statement.
5. Check your draft statement against the key questions for evaluating unit roles and missions listed in the next section. Force yourself to analyze the draft objectively. Invite others to assist you in the process.
6. Review the draft in depth with your immediate supervisor, your key employees, and any peer managers to whom it would be relevant. Modify the draft as appropriate.

Key Questions for Evaluating Unit Roles and Missions

The following questions should be used to validate or further modify your draft statement of unit roles and missions before final acceptance:

1. Does the statement include all *pertinent* commitments (for example, economic, functional, product, service, market, geographical)?

2. Is there a clear determination of production or support relationship?

3. Is the statement unique or distinctive in some way?

4. Is it consistent with, without duplicating, peer statements of roles and missions?

5. Is it understandable, brief, and concise?

6. Is the complete unit function stated and self-contained?

7. Does the statement provide a clear linkage to other related roles-and-missions statements?

What Are Some Examples of Unit Roles-and-Missions Statements?

The following examples are actual unit statements of roles and missions of specific departments in Burger King Corporation and BHP Minerals/The San Juan Mine (which are used here with permission), as well as other statements adapted from business and governmental organizations.

Burger King Operations Standards Department

Through the establishment, maintenance, and improvement of operational standards, the Operations Standards group will seek to

- Safeguard the Burger King® brand
- Enhance customer satisfaction
- Simplify restaurant operations
- Increase consistency
- Improve restaurant profitability

Burger King Worldwide Restaurant Operations—Latin America

In support of the Burger King® mission, Worldwide Restaurant Operations—Latin America will provide franchisees and restaurants with operational and marketing support. To accomplish this, we are committed to adding value by

- Assisting in building sales and profitability in existing and new restaurants that meet or exceed company and franchisee expectations
- Providing team leadership and open communication in ensuring high standards resulting in customer satisfaction
- Being sensitive and responsive to the cultural values and needs of the communities we serve
- Establishing and enhancing sound working relationships with suppliers and other business partners

Burger King Worldwide Restaurant Operations—Europe/Middle East/Africa (WWRO-EMA)

WWRO-EMA will provide the expertise and support to enable our franchisees and restaurants to deliver the Burger King® mission through a consistent and innovative approach to

- Improving customer satisfaction
- Increasing sales, profitability, and growth
- Ensuring high standards by improving restaurant operations
- Emphasizing teamwork, pan-EMA, amongst ourselves and our business partners

San Juan Mine Departments

Safety Department. To contribute to the mission and goals of San Juan Mine and BHP Minerals by serving as an expert resource on safety and health to all mine departments, ensuring compliance with MSHA [Mine Safety and Health Agency] and other appropriate regulatory agencies and coordinating the emergency response and chemical control programs. In support of this, we are committed to

- Providing up-to-date dynamic materials and resources for use in training in support of our mission
- Knowing, understanding, and serving our customers' needs in a timely manner
- Representing San Juan Mine and BHP Minerals on safety and health issues in the communities in which we are involved

Supply Department. To contribute to the mission and goals of San Juan Mine by ensuring cost-effective and timely purchase and distribution of required materials for internal customers. In support of this, we are committed to

- Knowing, understanding, and serving our customers' needs in a cost-effective and timely manner
- Creating and maintaining a work environment that encourages the growth and development of our employees
- Compliance with all regulatory and corporate requirements, while maintaining the highest standards of ethical performance

Engineering Department. To contribute to the mission and goals of San Juan Mine by providing innovative leadership to meet our customers' needs through effective design, planning, and technical support. In achieving this mission, our major roles are to

- Provide mine design and mine planning support
- Provide regulatory compliance design and planning support
- Provide surveying, drafting, and statistical support

- Provide strategic planning support for future growth
- Assist in the development of the technical and professional skills of staff
- Interact with external customers proactively and professionally
- Help make San Juan Mine an enjoyable place to work

Production Department. To contribute to the mission and goals of San Juan Mine by cost-effectively producing quality coal for our customers. In support of this, we are committed to

- Making safety first; production will follow
- Optimizing all production functions to support the production of quality coal
- Establishing and maintaining win-win relationships with all of our internal and external customers and suppliers
- Willing compliance with all regulatory requirements that apply to us
- Recognizing and improving the skills and performance of everyone in the department
- Creating an environment that encourages innovation and continuous improvement
- Being sensitive to the needs of the communities in which we operate

Maintenance Department. To contribute to the mission and goals of San Juan Mine by providing cost-effective quality maintenance service to our customers within an acceptable time frame. In support of this, we are committed to

- Making safety our first priority
- Complying with all regulatory requirements

- Establishing and maintaining win-win, trusting relationships with all of our internal and external customers and suppliers
- Clearly establishing expectations, recognizing individuals and holding them accountable for their performance
- Providing training and development opportunities to encourage all our employees to reach their full potential
- Continuous improvement through innovation, teamwork, training, planning, and cost management

Other Examples of Unit Roles and Missions

A *Marketing Department*. The roles and missions of the Marketing Department are to contribute to the profitability and growth of the ABC Corporation through the effective marketing and sales of its present and future products and services. These roles and missions will be carried out in the domestic industrial, educational, and governmental markets through direct sales and franchised dealers. This department exists in order to

- Pinpoint and maintain contact with widely scattered specialized markets throughout the United States
- Identify, qualify, and maintain contact with current and new influential buyers and decision makers in our markets
- Discover new uses and markets for existing products/services and to introduce new products/services effectively and economically
- Create a receptive audience for our products/services and for our sales representatives

A *Regional Office for a Federal Agency*. The roles and missions of the Southwest Area Office are to carry out the mission of the agency in our assigned geographical area by

- Continually assessing and responding to the related needs of the people and communities being served
- Effectively interpreting the agency's mission to those being served and to the general public
- Providing constructive feedback to the agency on local acceptance of agency programs and the need for new or modified services
- Ensuring cost-effective use of available resources
- Providing opportunities for meaningful and satisfying service and personal and career growth for all area employees

A Bank Operations Department. The roles and missions of the Operations Department are to contribute to the profitability and growth of the ABC Community Bank by providing high-quality services to the bank's customers in the following areas:

- Teller services
- Automated teller machine (ATM) services
- Bank-by-mail services
- Safe deposit services
- Contract collections
- New accounts
- Bookkeeping
- General ledger maintenance
- Monthly statements
- Cash maintenance and control
- Incoming and outgoing collections and transfers
- Clearings

The department exists in order to

- Provide bank customers with rapid, accurate, and courteous service designed to promote continuation and expansion of a banking relationship
- Protect the interests of the bank through cost-effective provision of services and by ensuring proper allocation of appropriate charges
- Promote and maintain a positive, helpful image for the bank with its customers and the general public
- Create and maintain a mutually supportive working and learning relationship among bank employees

In Summary

- A statement of unit roles and missions is an especially important document for you to develop prior to starting your unit's planning process.
- It needs to be in direct support of the mission statement for your total organization.
- Your roles-and-missions statement provides a foundation for clearly determining the efforts to be carried out at your unit level.
- Addressing the critical, ongoing expectations of your unit at least once a year helps to assure that the needs of the total organization will be met.

The next chapter will show you how to create a strategic vision for the total organization and will help you determine whether it is appropriate to create one for your unit as well.

CHAPTER SIX

What Should Be Your Future?

Creating Your Strategic Vision

Which comes first, mission or vision? This is almost like the "chicken and egg" situation. I can make an equally good case for going either way. However, since many of the questions posed in Chapters Four and/or Five, which you will be asking yourselves in connection with the development of your mission statement, have *visionary* implications, and since the definition of "mission" in this book has a broader interpretation than it does in many other books on strategic planning, I have chosen to deal with the development of vision *after* dealing with the development of mission. In fact, in my earlier writings, I incorporated vision as a part of mission, which may still be an appropriate posture for your organization. However, I have come to the conclusion fairly recently that for many organizations there is a value in separating the two, even though they are closely related.

What Is Vision and Why Is It Important?

As defined in Chapter One, *vision* is a representation of what you believe the future should look like for your organization in the eyes of your customers, employees, owners, and other important stakeholders. Vision is almost entirely *intuitive* in its origin. It is an outgrowth of the values and convictions of your management team. A well-stated vision statement:

- Is brief, preferably under ten words
- Is catchy and easy to remember

- Is inspiring and a challenge to future achievement
- Is believable and consistent with your strategic values and your mission
- Serves as a rallying point with all important stakeholders
- Clearly states the essence of what your organization must become
- Allows for flexibility and creativity in execution

James Collins and Jerry Porras present a legitimate caution in *Built to Last: Successful Habits of Visionary Companies*:

> It's become fashionable in recent decades for companies to spend countless hours and sums of money drafting elegant vision statements, values statements, mission statements, purpose statements, aspiration statements, objectives statements, and so on. Such pronouncements are all fine and good—indeed, they can be quite useful—but they're not the essence of a visionary company. *Just because a company has a "vision statement" (or something like it) in no way guarantees that it will become a visionary company!* If you walk away . . . thinking that the most essential step in building a visionary company is to write such a statement, then you will have missed the whole point. A statement might be a good first step, but it is *only* a first step.[1]

In their book *Strategic Readiness: The Making of the Learning Organization*, John Redding and Ralph Catalanello offer an interesting perspective on vision. They state that

> learning organizations seek to establish a clear strategic direction that is loose enough to allow for freedom of expression and creativity in execution. They have a vision that is constantly emerging and developing. A vision that embodies the essence of what the organization must become to survive in the future. A vision that, when compared against today's realities, necessitates continuing quests for

better ways. A vision that demonstrates that the organization is not a helpless victim of uncontrollable forces but an active agent that has some power over its own destiny. A vision that is kept purposely broad and open to allow for both the alteration of course over time and the involvement of the organization in the creation of the vision.[2]

In *Competing for the Future*, Gary Hamel and C. K. Prahalad prefer the concept of *foresight* to vision. "Industry foresight helps managers answer three questions. First, what new types of customer benefit should we seek to provide in five, ten, or fifteen years? Second, what new competencies will we need to build or acquire to offer those benefits to customers? And third, how will we need to reconfigure the customer interface over the next several years?"[3] They go on to comment about the disillusionment of some executives with "vision":

> Visions that are as grandiose as they are poorly conceived deserve to be criticized, as do companies that seem to prefer rhetoric to action. All too often, "the vision" is no more than window dressing for a CEO's ego-driven acquisition binge. . . . Any vision that is simply an extension of the CEO's ego is dangerous. On the other hand, it is equally simplistic and dangerous to reject the very notion of foresight simply because some corporate leaders can't distinguish between vanity and vision.[4]

One of Hamel and Prahalad's concepts that I particularly like is that of *core competencies*:

> To successfully compete for the future, a company must be capable of enlarging its *opportunity horizon*. This requires top management to conceive of the company as a portfolio of core competencies rather than a portfolio of individual business units. Business units are typically defined in terms of a specific product-market focus, whereas core competencies connote a broad class of customer

benefits (e.g., "user friendliness" at Apple, "pocketability" at Sony, or "untethered communications" at Motorola). . . . Any company that defines itself in terms of a specific set of end-product markets ties its fate to the fate of those particular markets. Markets mature, but competencies evolve.[5]

With that in mind, here are a few examples of evolving core competencies that may hold particular promise for your future. Your best list, however, is one that you develop yourself, allowing your creative imagination to run free.

Quick-responsiveness	Know-how in (specific)
Adaptability	technology
User-friendliness	Affordability
Reliability	Instant access
Customization	First-to-market
	Network marketing

One of the problems in establishing a generic label like *vision* is that its use will inevitably lead to misuse by some people. With all due respect to Hamel and Prahalad's perspectives (which are justified), I will predict that, should *foresight* become the industry term for a future point of view, it will not be long before there will be some glaring examples of misuse of that term. Therefore, for the time-being I will continue using *vision*.

How Do We Develop Our Vision Separately from Our Mission?

I will approach the development of your vision initially as an effort completely separate from the development of your mission. Later I will show you how you can develop it as a derivation of your mission.

The starting point with your vision, as with your mission, is the assessment of strategic values covered in Chapter Three. If you have completed that activity, review the priorities you have placed on these values and determine which ones need to be addressed in your vision. If you have not yet made that assessment, then you should do so before moving on.

Here are some questions designed to get each member of your management team thinking about how you should be looking at the future:

1. What do I see as the key to the future for our organization?
2. What unique contribution should we be making in the future?
3. What would make me excited about being a part of this organization in the future?
4. What values need to be stressed?
5. What are or should be our organization's core competencies?
6. What should be our positions on such things as customers, markets, profitability, growth, technology, quality, employees, and so on?
7. What do I see as our organization's greatest opportunity for growth?

For this effort to be effective, you and your management team need to allow your feelings to come out. As with mission development, this process needs to take place away from your organization's premises, in a setting where creative ideas can flow freely. Developing a vision is an intuitive, creative process. You need to respond to these questions initially as though you were looking at *the best of all possible worlds.* Assume that nothing is impossible. It's a lot easier to tone down an impractical or unrealistic statement than it is to expand one that is ultraconservative. Remember, you are creating a vision of what you would like your organization to become in the future, not necessarily an image of what it is today.

Once again, I urge you to use a skilled facilitator in this process that will be very similar to the process followed in developing your organization's mission. It includes:

1. Having team members write their answers to these questions (or a modified version of them) independently, in advance of your meeting, *without discussing their answers with other team members.* This enables the cogitative thinkers to be on equal footing with the spontaneous thinkers and encourages the sharing of differing points of view.

2. Having all team members share their answers to one question at a time at a meeting called for that purpose, with the answers posted on a flipchart or other visible recording instrument. The ground rules here are, of course, that no judgmental comments may be made about anyone's responses until all have been presented, although questions for clarification are permitted.

3. Discussing the answers to each question once everyone has responded, with the objective of reaching consensus (or as close to it as possible) on key words or phrases that reflect the organization's future perspective on that particular question. This can be one of the most creative discussions your team might have as you focus on factors that will challenge you to even greater heights.

4. Reviewing answers to all questions to reach agreement on the relatively few key words or phrases that need to be included in your vision statement.

5. Drafting a vision statement that meets the criteria identified at the beginning of this chapter. You can probably do this with your entire team participating since it is much briefer than your mission statement. However, having a few members of the team make an initial draft for review and modification by the total team is an option if time is limited.

6. Reviewing the draft with other key stakeholders, as done with the review of recommendations for your mission statement, to

make certain that others view it in the same light as the team that created it, making modifications as appropriate.

Figure 6.1 contains a few examples of vision statements that could have been developed through a process similar to this. Some of these examples are paraphrased versions of existing company statements while others are speculative. Yours should be original to you and a clear representation of your present and future commitments.

Figure 6.1 Sample Vision Statements

We will be seen as *the* high value supplier in each market we serve.

We will produce any product and enter any market where we can become a dominant supplier in our industry.

We will be the best merchandising company in our industry in terms of
- customer satisfaction
- individual store profitability

We will become a major global presence in our industry.

We are and will remain world-class in customer satisfaction and quality.

We will experience the joy that comes from the advancement, application, and innovation of technology that benefits humankind.

We will continually cheat yesterday's customers by being so much better tomorrow.

In our business, innovation, fun, and profit go hand in hand.

We want to be ⎫
We can be ⎬ THE BEST!
We will be ⎭

How Do We Develop Our Vision from Our Mission?

If you have already gone through the process of developing your mission and either have a draft statement or are in the process of developing one, then you may find it desirable to use the strategic thinking process you followed in creating your mission statement to develop your vision, without treating it as a separate effort.

Once again, you need to start by reviewing the priorities you set on your strategic values. Next, you need to go back over the answers that either you individually or the group came up with to the questions about clarifying your organization's mission presented in Figure 4.1 and/or the questions about unit roles and missions presented in Figure 5.1. Some of your answers may not be included in your mission statement, but they may provide some thoughts about what your vision of the future should be. The questions from Figure 4.1 that will be most useful are 1c, 1d, 2, 3, 4, 5, 6, 7, 9, and 11.

Review your draft mission statement and focus on those aspects of it that clearly focus on the future rather than on the present. A vision statement developed in conjunction with the mission statement will look very similar to one created separately, but it should be created with less effort since you will have already gone through much of the strategic thinking process.

How Do We Communicate Our Vision?

While it is important for all stakeholders to be familiar with your mission statement for decision-making purposes, your vision statement is the one they should remember and be inspired by. This is why it should conform to the criteria listed at the beginning of this chapter. Here is a shopping list of several ways that a vision statement can be either communicated or displayed:

- Letterheads
- Sales literature
- Annual reports
- News releases
- New employee orientations
- Employee handbooks
- Wall plaques
- Business cards

- Posters
- Paperweights
- Lucite-enclosed table pieces
- Staff meetings
- Criterion for new project determination
- Criterion for recruitment and selection of people
- Basis for interteam collaborative efforts

In Summary

- Your strategic vision is a representation of what you believe the future should look like for your organization in the eyes of your customers, employees, owners, and other important stakeholders.
- Your vision statement should be brief, catchy, easy to remember, inspiring, and a challenge to future achievement.
- It should focus on what you want to become, not necessarily on what you are now.
- It can be developed separately from or as a derivation of your mission statement.
- Your vision needs to be communicated or displayed in a wide variety of ways to ensure that it is remembered by and inspiring to your important stakeholders.

Chapter Seven shows you how to formulate your strategy to make certain that you are headed in the right strategic direction to support your mission and vision.

Notes

1. James C. Collins and Jerry I. Porras, *Built to Last: Successful Habits of Visionary Companies* (New York: HarperCollins, 1994), p. 201.
2. John C. Redding and Ralph F. Catalanello, *Strategic Readiness:*

The Making of the Learning Organization (San Francisco: Jossey-Bass, 1994), p. 179.

3. Gary Hamel and C. K. Prahalad, *Competing for the Future: Breakthrough Strategies for Seizing Control of Your Industry and Creating the Markets of Tomorrow* (Boston: Harvard Business School Press, 1994), p. 73.

4. Hamel and Prahalad, *Competing for the Future*, p. 75.

5. Hamel and Prahalad, *Competing for the Future*, p. 83.

CHAPTER SEVEN

Where Are You Going?

Formulating Your Strategy

The term *strategy* is used by some people to describe *how* something will be accomplished. Managers sometimes refer to their "strategies for penetrating a market" or "strategies for improving quality." I have never quite understood that use of the term since it runs contrary to my perception of strategy as that which defines where an organization is headed in the future rather than how it is going to get there. I will be using *strategy* in this book as *a process for determining the direction in which an organization needs to move to fulfill its mission*. This view sees strategy as primarily an intuitive process. I will concentrate much more on the *how* of getting there in the books on long-range and tactical planning.

What Is Strategy and Why Is It Important?

Strategy is a natural complement to mission and vision. First, you need to determine the concept of your organization, the nature of the business in which you are involved, why you exist, who you serve, the principles and values under which you intend to function, and what the future of your organization should look like. Next, you need to assess the direction in which you are currently headed to determine if that will be the most effective route to carrying out your mission and vision. What changes in direction may be indicated now? How and when will you make future decisions regarding your strategic direction? It will be the rare organization that will survive into the next century and beyond while continuing to function in the same way it has been functioning in the past.

The impact of rapidly changing technology, the global village, more sophisticated consumers, and increased competition (even in the public sector) makes the need for continual change a virtual necessity for most organizations. Such change could be, at one extreme, a radical departure from past practice, such as moving into an entirely different business. Or, at the other extreme, it could mean making a modest five-degree shift in direction.

Developing a clear strategy is important because it

- Provides you with a sound basis for making decisions that will keep you focused in the right direction
- Helps you avoid "rabbit trails" that may tempt you to move in the wrong direction
- Reinforces your mission and vision
- Leads to common agreement on direction from all contributing segments of your organization
- Saves time and effort
- Increases return on investment
- Increases interest on the part of stock/equity holders
- Provides a clear sense of direction to all important stakeholders

Hamel and Prahalad provide some interesting perspectives related to strategy. "To compete successfully for the future, senior managers must first understand just how competition for the future is different from competition for the present. The differences are profound. They challenge the traditional perspectives on strategy and competition. We will see that competing for the future requires not only a redefinition of strategy, but also a redefinition of top management's role in creating strategy."[1]

They have also introduced an insightful concept related to strategy, which they call *white spaces*.

When one conceives of a company as a portfolio of competencies, a whole new range of potential opportunities typically opens up. We use the term *white spaces* to refer to opportunities that reside between or around existing product-based business definitions. One example of a white space opportunity was the video art tablet that Sony created for children. The art tablet is, in essence, a detuned workstation graphics pad. With it, kids can use a television as a virtual coloring book. . . . Most companies work hard to delineate precisely unit-by-unit ownership of existing market space, but shouldn't equal attention be given to assigning responsibility for white spaces? Too often white spaces are orphans.[2]

What opportunities do you have that might lie just outside the boundaries of *the obvious?*

How Should We Approach Strategy?

Henry Mintzberg, one of the truly brilliant seminal thinkers of our time, has written a provocative book published in 1994 called *The Rise and Fall of Strategic Planning.* In it, he both highlights and frequently debunks some of the more popular approaches to strategy and strategic planning. His position is that strategic planning as many authors present it is primarily an *analytical* process, whereas strategy, to be effective, needs to be much more *intuitive.* He comments that

the strategy hierarchy is conventionally described to flow from corporate strategies (intentions concerning the portfolio of businesses) to business strategies (intentions concerning marketing, production, sourcing, etc.). The assumption apparent in the strategic planning model is that all of this is put into question each time the exercise is undertaken, typically annually, on a well-defined schedule, starting with corporate strategies at the top and working down. There is, however, no reason to believe that strategies should, can, or actually do change on a regular schedule, let alone an annual one. Indeed, all evidence . . . is to the contrary: real strategic change is ad hoc and irregular, with strategies often remaining stable over long periods of time and then suddenly changing all at once.[3]

Mintzberg's insights are one of the reasons I decided to separate *strategic thinking* from *long-range planning* in this series.

While I might challenge a few of the positions Mintzberg takes, I agree wholeheartedly that you cannot proceduralize strategic thinking any more than you can legislate morality. However, I believe there are structures that can be put in place that will enable you and your management team to be more creative in establishing your future direction without losing your ability to respond effectively to changing circumstances. I will share two approaches to creating these structures. The first is an updated version of the *driving force* approach my coauthors Patrick Below and Betty Acomb and I presented in our 1987 book, *The Executive Guide to Strategic Planning*. The second approach will be a simplified *questioning* approach that expands on your answers to the questions posed about mission and vision in Chapters Four, Five, and Six. If you are interested in exploring other approaches, please refer to some of the books listed in the Annotated Resources section at the back of this book.

The Driving Force Approach

I first came across the concept of the *driving force* in Benjamin Tregoe and John Zimmerman's 1980 book *Top Management Strategy*. I found this concept to be a major contribution to helping my clients focus on determining their strategic direction. My coauthors and I subsequently presented a similar approach in *The Executive Guide to Strategic Planning*, drawing on the Tregoe and Zimmerman perspectives (with their permission) and adding some of our own. The concept has evolved, as it should, based on my experience in working with clients. The approach I will share here contains some of the same perspectives included in both of the referenced books plus some variations that have worked with some of my clients. (Tregoe and Zimmerman, together with two of their Kepner-Tregoe colleagues, Ronald Smith and Peter Tobia, also came out with an updated version of the driving force approach in their 1989 book *Vision in Action*, which is described in the Annotated Resources.)

Strategy formulation is a necessary precursor to long-range planning, to keep that part of the planning process from being almost exclusively an extrapolation of history. Without a strategy in place, managers frequently end up making decisions based on operational or tactical rather than strategic perspectives. To quote Tregoe and Zimmerman's first book, "The operations palliative, if taken alone, is dangerous medicine for treating a crisis or change which could threaten the survival of the business. If an organization is headed in the wrong direction, the last thing it needs is to get there more efficiently. And if an organization is headed in the right direction, it surely does not need to have that direction unwittingly changed by operational action taken in a strategic void."[4]

Taking this approach will help you to

1. Define and determine the discrete strategic factors that affect the direction of your organization

2. Establish these factors in priority order

3. Determine your organization's driving force, both present and future

4. Identify changes that must take place if a new direction is indicated

5. Formulate a strategy statement that establishes a clear direction for your organization

Let me define how I will be using the term *driving force* before moving on to describe the process. The concept of the driving force, as espoused by Tregoe and Zimmerman, has been a significant contribution to strategy formulation. They define the driving force as "the primary determiner of the scope of future products and markets."[5] I have expanded this concept slightly, defining it as *the primary factor impacting all major decisions affecting the future of your organization.* Other factors will represent important considerations but, when the final decision is made, there needs to be one factor that will be the most decisive. This is your driving force.

1. **Defining and determining your strategic factors,** those that are likely to have a major impact on how your future business decisions will be made, is an important first step. As you evaluate the products or services you should be offering to the marketplace and the markets you should be serving in the future, you need to determine what major factors will most affect your decisions. Clients I have worked with have identified six primary factors that appear on most of their lists plus several others that are relevant to some. I will describe each of these factors briefly so you can determine which are most relevant to your organization. I will then show you a process for prioritizing them.

Primary Factors

• *Products Offered.* This strategic factor is important in an organization that produces specific classes of products and/or services which it then offers to the markets it serves. It may expand into other markets interested in such products and may offer some customization to attract additional customers. However, an organization with this factor as its driving force will focus most of its efforts on continuing to produce the products that represent its core business, updating them regularly to take advantage of changing technology and to respond to customer demands. Companies in the automotive industry typically are quite strongly influenced by this factor.

• *Market Needs.* An organization focusing on this factor typically has established or is in the process of establishing strong relationships with specific markets and customer groupings. It is continually assessing their needs to determine how best to serve them, which could include the development of new products and services that may have significantly different characteristics from those the organization has traditionally produced and that will expand its business in those markets. Systems development companies frequently place strong emphasis on this factor.

• *Return/Profit.* Every organization, whether in the private or public sector, must generate more income than expenses or it will not stay in business for long. Whether that positive difference is called profit, return, reserves, or some other appropriate term, it is essential to organizational survival. That importance does not make it the organization's driving force, however. An organization with return/profit as its driving force is one that will engage in virtually any undertaking within its broad business umbrella that will produce a minimum strategically preset return. Conversely, with a few exceptions, it will divest itself of any business that does not consistently provide that preset return. While all organizations must have a return/profit motive, for most, other strategic factors will have greater impact on future decisions. Large diverse financial holding companies are more likely than other businesses to have return/profit as their primary strategic factor or driving force.

• *Size/Growth.* While related to return/profit, size/growth as a strategic factor is focused on an organization's desire to reach a particular size or sustain a particular rate of growth in order to enhance its market position, to attain a *critical mass* that will give it an advantage over its competition, or to preempt an opportunity during change in the industry. Companies desiring to position themselves either to make a public stock offering or to be an attractive merger or acquisition candidate might also select size/growth as their driving force. Generally, a size/growth strategy is a temporary one that will take on a lesser role once the organization's primary goals have been reached.

• *Technology.* The focus here is on the organization that sees its competitive advantage related to its ability to either create or quickly respond to significant technological advances and/or to be perceived as a technological leader in its field. It is an organization that is willing to make the investment and take the risks required to reach and maintain that position. Certain companies in the pharmaceutical industry are examples of organizations with technology as a primary factor or driving force.

• *Human Resources.* Many organizations view their human assets as being their most valuable resource. Consequently, they will look for future opportunities that will either capitalize on the capabilities their people bring to the table or enhance their ability to attract and retain the calibre of people they wish to have in their organizations. Organizations selecting this as a primary factor might include certain high-tech companies as well as some large specialized consulting organizations.

Other Potential Factors

- *Services Offered.* This is a variation on the *Products Offered* factor for those organizations whose principal deliverables to their customers are human effort, including but not limited to such things as financial services, information services, medical and legal services, repair and maintenance, training, and the like. Products provided, if any, are incidental to the services provided. This is a major factor impacting my consulting practice.

- *Customer Needs.* This is a variation on *Market Needs* that is applicable to an organization that has a predetermined and finite group of customers and for which expansion of the customer base is limited, such as a utility. Business expansion is dependent largely on increasing sales of new deliverable products and services in response to the needs of the particular customer base.

- *Service Capability.* This is identified as a strategic factor when the products or services an organization delivers are heavily dependent on the support services provided and the sources of such services are limited. Any expansion into new products or markets would be compromised unless the infrastructure and human and technical capabilities were in place to provide that support. Conversely, an organization with a surplus of such capability may be looking for expanded opportunities where that capability could be leveraged. An example of an organization for which this might be a major factor is a gourmet restaurant chain. (Where would it be without a sufficient number of gourmet chefs?)

- *Production Capacity.* Similar to *Service Capability*, this factor would be important for an organization with a heavy investment in capital equipment, processes, or systems. Such an organization might wish to limit any expansion to what it could handle with existing capacity, look for ways to make more productive use of this capacity, or assess the potential return on additional capital investment. A company such as a metal fabrication company is likely to focus on this factor.

- *Method of Sale/Distribution.* Companies with unique or distinctive sales or distribution capabilities might wish to look at additional products or markets for which that would be an advantage. This is a significant consideration for home shopping networks and warehouse membership organizations.

- *Natural Resources.* This is a useful factor for organizations that either own or control certain natural resources. They look for ways of leveraging that advantage. Petroleum and land-management organizations are examples of companies that are likely to address this factor.

- *Organizational Image.* Some organizations have worked very hard at establishing and maintaining a specific image in the marketplace, the industry in which they are represented, or the communities in which they operate. Consequently, they would want to make certain that any new products or markets they are considering would enhance rather than detract from that image. My own business is a classic example of one in which this is an important strategic factor. My decision to focus on providing high-level expertise in the field of strategic and tactical planning keeps me from engaging in other types of business that might weaken that image.

2. Establishing your strategic factors in priority order can be done very effectively using a process of *paired comparisons.* The purpose of this process is to determine which strategic factors will have the greatest influence on decisions affecting the future of your organization and, specifically, which one will be your driving force, the one factor that will be the ultimate determinant of whether you should proceed in a particular strategic direction.

The method for determining your driving force is relatively simple, but it is powerful as a means of bringing out differing points of view in a constructive manner with the expectation that a consensus can be reached. It's especially important to have a skilled facilitator who does not have a strong personal bias toward one factor lead the team in this consensus effort.

• The first step is for your team members to reach agreement on which strategic factors need to be considered. I recommend starting with the primary factors identified earlier in this chapter, determining if all are applicable or if some could be eliminated as not being relevant to your business. Next take a look at the other potential factors and determine which of these need to be considered and which would have little or no significant impact on your decision making. There may also be some additional strategic factors unique to your business that should be included on your list. This selection process should move fairly quickly since discussion at this stage is limited to whether each factor belongs on the list to be considered and does not include consideration of its relative importance compared with that of others. That comes next.

• Once your team has reached consensus on which factors need to be considered, these factors are entered on the horizontal lines on a *decision matrix,* such as the one shown in Figure 7.1 (which includes the primary factors; other relevant factors need to be added). These factors are entered once more on the vertical lines under the same numbers at the top of each column. This matrix may be prepared and distributed to team members in advance of your planning meeting with instructions to complete it on their own prior to participating in the consensus effort. The matrix may also be prepared on a flipchart, transparency, computer screen, or other display medium where it can be viewed by the entire group while the consensus effort is proceeding. (Note: although the decision matrix is a copyrighted instrument, you have my permission to duplicate it as long as the copyright identification is included.)

• Your facilitator will establish the criteria by which the discussion of strategic factors will proceed. You will be comparing two factors at a time, making a judgment about the relative importance of each, using the criteria established. The major criterion I generally use at this point is *impact on decisions affecting the future direction of the organization.* Other criteria, such as ones related to product or market development, may be more appropriate to your organization.

Once you have agreed on criteria, you will compare one *horizontal factor* with one *vertical factor* at a time and make a choice as a team regarding which of the two is more important, using the criteria selected. For example, if you were comparing *Products Offered* to *Market Needs* and you reached a consensus decision that *Products Offered* should have greater impact on decisions affecting the future of your organization, you would place an X in the box on the matrix where these two factors converge. If you decided that *Market Needs* should have greater impact, you would leave that box blank. (An X in the box indicates the horizontal factor is more important; a blank box indicates the vertical factor is more important.) When a decision is reached on one comparison, you move on to comparing the same horizontal factor to the next vertical factor, continuing to the end of the first line, then moving on to the second horizontal factor. (The shaded area on the matrix keeps you from comparing one factor against itself and from comparing two factors more than once.) By the time you reach the end of the last horizontal line, you will have compared every factor on your list with every other factor *once* and made a choice. If you have been consistent in your application of your criteria, the rest is simple arithmetic. You add the number of X's marked on each horizontal line and the number of blank boxes in each vertical line; then add the two totals together and your strategic factors should fall out in rank order of importance. If two or more factors end up with the same total, it indicates a slight inconsistency in your application of the criteria. The easiest way to correct that is to do a simple ranking of such items. Figure 7.2 illustrates a completed decision matrix used with one of my clients. (Their reasons for selecting one factor over another are not important to the illustration.) The actual rank order of the factors is shown at the bottom of the figure.

While this may appear to be a somewhat mechanical process, I can assure you it is not. Team discussions while comparing two factors can range from a quick decision, because everyone is in obvious

Figure 7.1 Strategic Areas Decision Matrix

	1	2	3	4	5	6	7	8	9	10	11	12	13	14	Total X's
	Products Offered	Market Needs	Return/Profit	Size/Growth	Technology	Human Resources									
1 Products Offered															1
2 Market Needs															2
3 Return/Profit															3
4 Size/Growth															4
5 Technology															5
6 Human Resources															6
7															7
8															8
9															9
10															10
11															11
12															12
13															13
14															14
	1	2	3	4	5	6	7	8	9	10	11	12	13	14	
Vertical (blank boxes)															
Horizontal (X's)															
Total															
Rank Order															

Instructions

1. Review list of areas and eliminate any that do not apply; add any others that may be appropriate on the blank lines, repeating each under the corresponding number at the top.
2. Evaluate #1 against #2. If #1 is **more important**, place X in box under #2; if #1 is **less important**, leave blank. Repeat with **each** remaining number. Continue to next line; repeat.
3. **Total X's across** for each number; enter in *Horizontal box* at bottom; **total blank boxes down** for each; enter in *Vertical box* at bottom; **add both** *Horizontal* and *Vertical* for *Total.*
4. **Largest** number under *Total* will be #1 in *Rank order;* **next largest** will be #2, and so on. If two or more have the same *Total*, compare each subjectively against the others.

Copyright 1995 by Jossey-Bass Publishers, San Francisco. From *Morrisey on Planning: A Guide to Strategic Thinking,* by George L. Morrisey. Permission to reproduce is hereby granted.

Figure 7.2 Strategic Areas Decision Matrix (Example)

	1 Products Offered	2 Market Needs	3 Return/Profit	4 Size/Growth	5 Technology	6 Human Resources	7 Customer Needs	8 Service Capability	9 Organizational Image	10	11	12	13	14	Total X's	
1 Products Offered								X	X						2	1
2 Market Needs			X	X		X	X	X	X						6	2
3 Return/Profit				X				X	X						3	3
4 Size/Growth								X	X						2	4
5 Technology						X	X	X	X						4	5
6 Human Resources							X	X	X						3	6
7 Customer Needs								X	X						2	7
8 Service Capability															0	8
9 Organizational Image															0	9
10																10
11																11
12																12
13																13
14																14

	1	2	3	4	5	6	7	8	9	10	11	12	13	14
Vertical (blank boxes)	0	1	1	1	4	3	3	0	1					
Horizontal (X's)	2	6	3	2	4	3	2	0	0					
Total	2	7	4	3	8	6	5	0	1					
Rank Order	7	2	5	6	1	3	4	9	8					

1. Technology
2. Market Needs
3. Human Resources
4. Customer Needs
5. Return/Profit
6. Size/Growth
7. Products Offered
8. Organizational Image
9. Service Capability

agreement, to an extended sharing of different viewpoints before a choice is made. It's important to allow sufficient time for such discussion, which can be very productive in clarifying your team's perspective since you will be focusing on comparing just two factors at a time. Should the discussion become bogged down, particularly when one or two people resist consensus, your facilitator may need to force a decision to keep the process moving.

3.   *Determining your organization's driving force, both present and future*, is the next step. Having identified your organization's strategic factors and placed them in rank order related to their *impact on decisions affecting the future of the organization* (or whatever criteria you have selected), you can now test the validity of the process you went through with the decision matrix. The number one factor on your list becomes your organization's future driving force, with the next three or four factors representing major decision influencers.

You need to be alert to one major consideration in reaching agreement. Many managers start out believing that *Return/Profit* is their organization's driving force. My experience in working with clients indicates that this is seldom true. While as indicated earlier every organization, whether in the private or public sector, must generate more income than expenses in order to remain in business, that fact does not make this every organization's driving force. With the possible exception of financial holding companies, one or more of the other factors almost always turn out to provide greater impact on most organizations' future decision making. By accepting the fact that a positive return is essential to survival, we can then move on to examining the relative importance of these other factors. Suggesting that *Return/Profit*, or any other strategic factor, is not the driving force is not relegating it to a position of unimportance. It is merely placing it in proper perspective with other factors being considered.

4.   *Identifying changes that must take place if a new direction is indicated* establishes a basis for developing strategies for the future. Having determined your future driving force and your other high-impact strategic factors, you next need to determine if these factors are significantly different from the driving force and other factors that have influenced your decisions up until now. You may wish to go through the decision matrix once more using *impact on*

current major decisions as your criterion. One possible conclusion may be that the strategic course you are already following, consciously or intuitively, is the appropriate one for the future as well. (Caution: be careful not to slip into this conclusion too easily or you may find yourselves lagging behind on changes that need to take place.) You are more likely, however, to reach a conclusion that a different direction is necessary to optimize your organization's journey into the future.

Using the insights gained through your efforts in defining your mission and your vision as well as in prioritizing your strategic factors and determining your driving force, your response, individually and collectively, to the following questions will help you formulate your strategy:

- What should be our future driving force? Why?
- What other strategic factors should have impact on major decisions affecting our future? Why?
- How do these factors differ from our current driving force and/or strategic factors affecting our current strategic decisions?
- What changes need to be addressed to meet the requirements of our future driving force?
- How are these conclusions compatible with our mission and vision?
- What elements of our mission and vision need to be addressed in our strategy?

5. *Formulating a strategy statement that establishes a clear direction for your organization* is a natural outgrowth of this process. The format of your strategy statement may look similar to the format recommended for your mission statement. However, it serves a somewhat different purpose. Here is a suggested format for your strategy statement, although the wording may vary, as the two later examples will show:

- *Proposed statement of strategy:*

- *For this to happen, the following need to take place:*

It is possible to reach the conclusion that your mission statement addresses strategy sufficiently, providing a strong enough focus for future direction. However, I recommend that you go through the process of strategy formulation before jumping to that conclusion. As with all elements of strategic thinking, the process is more important than the product. Here is an example of a strategy statement for Auspex Systems, a public corporation located in Santa Clara, California, that used a variation on the driving force approach (Auspex's mission statement is shown in Chapter Four):

> Auspex Systems Customer Needs/Satisfaction Driving Force establishes that future decisions on new products and/or markets to invest in will be based on the following criteria in descending order of importance:
>
> - Our ability to achieve world-class recognition in customer satisfaction and quality
> - Our leveragability in relation to current products and product families and our use of or contribution to our core technology base
> - Our responsiveness to identified needs within our targeted market segments
> - Our ability to meet our profitability targets

The Questioning Approach

This approach is most useful when you do not anticipate any significant controversy around strategic factors such as those described in the driving force approach. It is also based on the assumption that you have completed your efforts related to strategic values, mission, and vision or are in the process of doing so. The purpose of the questioning approach is to expand on the discussions held in connection with these previous efforts, resulting in a consensus on the conclusions or strategies that will help prepare a foundation for your long-range and tactical planning efforts. As in previous efforts, a skilled facilitator will help keep the process moving.

In preparation for a session to develop strategy, I recommend the completion of answers to the following questions. Naturally, these questions may be modified, additional ones added and some deleted to make them more relevant to your organization. Some of the questions are similar to ones addressed in mission and vision development. As in earlier questioning processes, I recommend that participants complete their answers individually prior to your planning meeting. This will ensure that participants will be mentally prepared for the meeting and that those who prefer to reflect on their thinking will be able to contribute on an equal footing with those who are more spontaneous in their thinking.

1. What do you see as the major trends in the industries or sectors that we currently serve or should be serving in the future?
2. Who are the customers we are likely to be serving in the future? How do they differ from today's customers?
3. How will we reach our customers in the future?
4. Who are likely to be our competitors in the future?
5. What aspects of our business do you believe have the greatest potential for growth in the future?
6. What aspects of business should we be involved in five to ten years in the future that we are not involved in currently?
7. What aspects of our current business should be reduced or eliminated over the next five to ten years?
8. What human and technical competencies need to be created or expanded in order to meet the challenges of the future?

9. What would make this an exciting and challenging organization in five to ten years?

10. If you were starting your career now, what would make you want to be a part of our organization's future?

11. Which of our strategic values will require concentrated effort on our part over the next several years if we are to continue to grow as a viable enterprise?

The primary value in going through this process lies in the opportunity for members of your management team to share their dreams about the future of your organization in a somewhat structured setting. The questions are designed to focus on where you are going rather than on where you are. Without a structure to force strategic thinking, it is all too easy to remain involved in day-to-day operations until it is too late to make the necessary changes. Here is an example of a strategy statement largely derived using the *questioning* approach for Atwood Mobile Products, a privately owned company whose headquarters are in Rockford, Illinois (Atwood's mission statement is shown in Chapter Four):

> The strategy of Atwood Mobile Products is to pursue new products and markets where we can dominate and which will lead to increased growth and profitability. For this to happen, we will
>
> • Develop new products that meet the needs of our current and future markets through increased customer partnering
>
> • Increase recognition of the Atwood name by consumers and customers as the standard of excellence for quality and convenience
>
> • Continually improve our responsiveness to customers' requirements
>
> • Develop a dominant position in Europe
>
> • Develop Product Management Teams and internal champions
>
> • Develop additional niche markets
>
> • Promote the recreation lifestyle

When Do We Change Our Strategy?

You change your strategy whenever you determine that the one you are following is no longer likely to lead you in the appropriate direction or if a new strategy emerges that clearly has greater potential for carrying out your mission and vision. Once you have determined an appropriate strategy, however, you will have made a significant investment of both tangible resources and emotional commitment. Therefore, strategy should not be changed casually. (You will find the critical issue analysis process described in the book on long-range planning especially helpful in assessing whether a change in strategy is appropriate.)

Echoing my earlier quote from Mintzberg, strategy does not change on a regular schedule. You need to be alert to opportunities and threats that may impact your strategy and be prepared to address them when they appear. However, I also recommend formally reviewing your strategy at least once a quarter to determine if it is still valid or if it needs to be modified or even changed completely if new information or circumstances justify. And, as a part of your annual strategic planning process, you need to formally revisit your strategy to see what changes might be appropriate.

In Summary

- Strategy is a process for determining the direction in which your organization needs to move to fulfill its mission.

- It addresses where you are headed in the future, not how you are going to get there.

- It requires you to look beyond the obvious for new and creative ways to meet the competitive challenges you will be facing in the future.

- It can be addressed through an assessment and prioritization of the strategic factors likely to impact all major decisions affecting the future of your organization.

- It can also be addressed through a series of open-ended questions designed to expand your thinking about where your organization should be headed.

- It needs to be reviewed regularly to determine whether it is still valid or if further change is in order.

- It is a necessary precursor to long-range planning to keep that part of the planning process from being almost exclusively an extrapolation of history.

- It is the final step in the strategic thinking portion of the planning process.

The next, and final, chapter in this book will show you how to pull your strategic thinking efforts together so you can proceed more effectively with your long-range and tactical planning efforts.

Notes

1. Gary Hamel and C. K. Prahalad, *Competing for the Future: Breakthrough Strategies for Seizing Control of Your Industry and Creating the Markets of Tomorrow* (Boston: Harvard Business School Press, 1994), p. 30.
2. Hamel and Prahalad, *Competing for the Future*, p. 84.
3. Henry Mintzberg, *The Rise and Fall of Strategic Planning: Reconceiving Roles for Planning, Plans, Planners* (New York: Free Press, 1994), pp. 74–75.
4. Benjamin B. Tregoe and John W. Zimmerman, *Top Management Strategy: What It Is and How to Make It Work* (New York: Simon and Schuster, 1980), p. 19.
5. Tregoe and Zimmerman, *Top Management Strategy*, p. 40.

CHAPTER EIGHT

What Happens Next?

Building a Bridge to the Rest of Your Planning Process

Strategic thinking is primarily an *intuitive* process. By itself, it is little more than an interesting intellectual exercise. Yet without it, your subsequent planning efforts will lack the focus needed to make them truly effective. Strategic thinking provides the foundation from which you can make meaningful planning decisions. It establishes a benchmark against which these decisions can be evaluated before plunging ahead into what may be activity without direction. It is also a powerful process for bringing your management team closer together as they help create your organization's future.

What Do We Do with the Results of Our Strategic Thinking?

The results of your strategic thinking will incorporate the decisions you have reached related to strategic values, organization or unit mission, vision, and strategy. You may wish to have separate statements for all four of these elements, although I find that a bit cumbersome. At the other extreme, you may be able to combine them all in a single comprehensive mission statement. You need to decide what format will serve your purposes most effectively. Your statements must be easily accessible to and understood by all those who must relate to them.

Regardless of whether you have a single statement or two or more separate statements, I strongly recommend that *they be included on a single sheet of paper*. There are two primary reasons for this: First, it forces brevity; the shorter and crisper your statements are, the more useful they will be. Second, a single sheet of paper is easier to refer to as a guide for decision making.

Throughout the strategic thinking process you have been encouraged to share your draft efforts with others, inviting their inputs and feedback. This collaboration needs to continue after you have completed your initial efforts. You probably will not be completely satisfied with your initial results and may be tempted to keep the document under wraps until you have completed your fine tuning. In my judgment, this would be a mistake. I believe you would be better off releasing a document that is 90 to 95 percent satisfactory, with the understanding that it will be subject to review and possible modification at some designated time in the future, such as in six months. Let your people understand your strategic thinking and use the document as a guide for a period of time. Make sure they understand that the document states the way you intend to function for the foreseeable future but that it may be modified based on "real world" experience in using it. The true test of its effectiveness occurs when your employees and other important stakeholders see that you are practicing what you have preached and they are doing the same.

Are We Ready to Proceed with Long-Range Planning?

Long-range planning has *future positioning* as its principal focus. It takes the *perspectives* you have developed through your strategic thinking and translates them into a projection of where you need to be at some point in the future in order to fulfill your mission. While a three- to five-year horizon is typical for many organizations, this period could be significantly longer or somewhat shorter for you, depending on the nature of your business. Ironically, if you have made a five-year projection, I predict with almost absolute certainty that you will end up at a different position in five years. *This does not invalidate the long-range planning process.* Intervening circumstances are likely to cause you to lengthen, shorten, or change the positions you have projected. The value of having a long-range plan is to provide you with a template that you can use to evaluate those intervening circumstances and make a judgment as to whether a change is justified. In order to respond more appropriately to a changing marketplace, new technology, fluctuations in the economy, and other such considerations, you need to have the latitude to pursue additional options while still maintaining your strategic vision. This is why I strongly recommend establishing a *rolling* long-range plan that is updated at least once a year or at any time a significant change in direction is indicated.

The second book in this series, *A Guide to Long-Range Planning: Creating Your Strategic Journey*, provides a structure for developing and implementing a long-range plan. The long-range planning process is a blend of intuition and analysis. You may make some projections about where you would like to be without necessarily knowing how you will get there. Part of the purpose of long-range planning is to take some of the dreams generated through your strategic thinking and translate them into desired future positions. This dreaming will be tempered by some analysis that will help you focus on the areas and issues that will have the greatest impact on creating your organization's future.

Long-range planning has four primary elements:

1. *Key Strategic Areas* help you to segment future positions into broad categories such as Future Markets, Future Products, Human Competencies, and Capital Expansion. This enables you to focus your attention on those strategic issues that will have the greatest impact on the future of your organization.

2. *Critical Issue Analysis* helps you to both validate and analyze your strategic issues to increase the probability that future efforts you put forth will keep you moving in the right direction.

3. *Long-Term Objectives* represent the future positions you wish to attain. Typically, they describe what you want to "have" or to "become" at designated future times in order to carry out

your mission, vision, and strategy. They also include your financial projections.

4. *Strategic Action Plans* focus on the major blocks of effort that will need to be expended to reach your long-term objectives. These plans normally require cross-functional effort and are incremental in nature. They are your principal bridge to your tactical plans.

Your long-range planning efforts generally will be concentrated during the first and second quarters of your fiscal year and will be a natural outgrowth of your strategic thinking efforts. However, you may need to address your long-range plan throughout your fiscal year either through a normal review process or when a major event occurs that requires a reassessment of your plan.

Are We Ready to Proceed with Tactical Planning?

Tactical planning takes the *perspectives* determined through your strategic thinking and the *positions* projected in your long-range planning and translates them into short-term *performance*. Do you need to complete your strategic thinking and long-range planning before proceeding with your tactical planning? No! Will your tactical planning be more effective if you have completed them first? Yes! Is it desirable to go through the strategic thinking process before doing tactical planning, even if you do not plan to develop your long-range plan right away? Yes! Tactical planning is much more *analytical* than *intuitive*, however, with its emphasis on practical, measurable results.

Many reasonably successful organizations perform quite well by putting most of their efforts into a short-term tactical planning process. The problem with this, of course, is that your planning efforts tend to be *reactive* to what is taking place rather than *proactive* toward where you should be heading. Tactical planning is an ongoing process even though you may place most of your formal effort into the latter part of your fiscal year as you prepare for the following year. Tactical planning goes on daily as you address both new and recurring short-term issues. A strong strategic foundation, however, will make that ongoing process much more productive.

The third book in this series, *A Guide to Tactical Planning: Producing Your Short-Term Results*, will show you how to function using six primary elements:

1. *Key Results Areas* represent those priority areas within which you need to achieve *results* during the projected planning period, including such areas as financial results, sales performance, customer service, and new product development. At the unit level, they could include such things as quality improvement, productivity, cost control, and employee morale.

2. *Critical Issue Analysis* helps you to validate and analyze short-term issues drawn from three primary sources:

    Your organization's strategic or long-range plan

    Your current year's plan and performance on issues that will carry over into your next plan year

    Other issues, current problems, or opportunities likely to impact your organization during the projected plan year

3. *Key Performance Indicators* are measurable factors within each of your key results areas on which you may wish to set specific objectives.

4. *Objectives* represent the specific measurable results to be accomplished within the time span of your plan.

5. *Action Plans* represent the actions required to accomplish each objective, including specific time frames, resource requirements, and accountability for each step.

6. *Plan Review* closes the loop in the planning process by ensuring that what you set out to accomplish actually gets translated into action that leads to results.

When and How Do We Reassess Our Strategic Thinking?

There are three primary times when it is important to reassess your strategic thinking:

1. *Whenever you are facing major opportunities or threats or a major change in structure* (as with a merger or acquisition), you must make certain that your projected actions are consistent with your stated philosophy. If there appears to be a significant discrepancy between the two, you need to either reconsider your projected actions or modify your stated philosophy to bring them into harmony.

2. *Annually*, at the start of your planning cycle, you need to reassess your strategic values, mission, vision, and strategy to ascertain whether your philosophy and your actions are still compatible and whether any significant change in perspective is called for. If change is indicated, you need to be prepared to make the necessary modifications. Strategy needs to be reviewed in depth at least once a year with modifications made as appropriate. Values, mission, and vision need to at least be reviewed to make sure they are current. I also recommend that you go through the process of determining your values and developing your mission and vision *at least once every three or four years—as though no such statements exist.* The process itself is a valuable exercise in team building and provides an opportunity to think creatively about who you are and where you are going. Remember, *the process is more important than the product.*

3. *At designated times throughout the year,* usually once a quarter, to keep your stated philosophy fresh and to be certain that your ongoing actions are consistent with your mission, vision, and strategy.

In Summary

- The results of your strategic thinking will incorporate the decisions you have reached related to strategic values, organization or unit mission, vision, and strategy.

- These results may be combined in a single statement or in two or more separate statements.

- They should be included on a single sheet of paper to force brevity and to make them easier to refer to as a guide for decision making.

- They provide the perspectives from which you can determine the future positions you wish to attain as a part of your long-range planning.

- They provide the foundation that will enable you to make sound decisions related to the short-term performance required in your tactical plan.

Figure 8.1 reiterates the complete planning process, including the three components and their elements. While each component can stand alone, each will be enhanced by integrating them into a total process. With your strategic thinking clarified, you may now proceed with the balance of your strategic planning effort, which will be described in the second book in this series, *A Guide to Long-Range Planning: Creating Your Strategic Journey*; or, if your planning need is more immediate, you may wish to proceed to a short-term planning effort as described in the third book in this series, *A Guide to Tactical Planning: Producing Your Short-Term Results*.

If you don't know where you are going, any road will take you there is the truism with which I started this book. I trust I have succeeded in providing you with a process for determining your strategic direction so you can make certain you are on the *right* road for a successful journey.

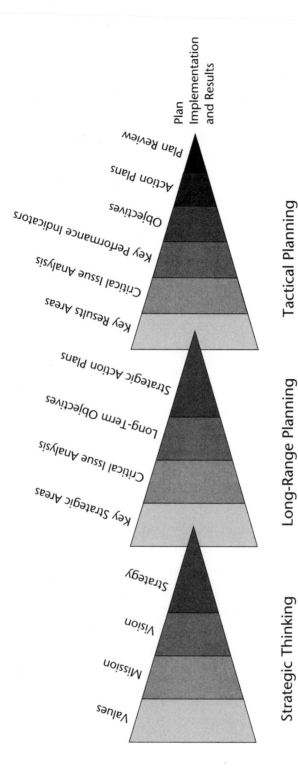

Values

Mission

Vision

Strategy

Strategic Thinking

Key Strategic Areas

Critical Issue Analysis

Long-Term Objectives

Strategic Action Plans

Long-Range Planning

Key Results Areas

Critical Issue Analysis

Key Performance Indicators

Objectives

Action Plans

Plan Review

Plan Implementation and Results

Tactical Planning

Figure 8.1 The Planning Process

Annotated Resources

I have found the following books useful in my study of management and planning practices. Most are recent publications, but I have also included a few classics that have influenced me greatly as I have proceeded on my own journey through the world of planning. This is not an exhaustive list. There are many other fine publications; these just happen to be ones that are meaningful to me. Since the subject matter of many of these titles overlaps the content in each of the three books in this series, the same set of annotated resources appears in each of them.

General Management and Management Tools

Applegate, Jane. *Strategies for Small Business Success*. New York: Plume/Penguin, 1995.

> This delightful book by a nationally syndicated columnist is both a compilation of some of her most popular columns and a collection of advice gathered from many small business entrepreneurs as well as from her own experience. The section on "Going Global" is especially worth reading by those who are anticipating moving into foreign markets.

Batten, Joe D. *Tough-Minded Leadership*. New York: Amacom, 1989.

> Joe Batten has been a close friend and colleague of mine for many years. As a writer and speaker, he has a unique talent for getting people to practice what they profess to believe. This book is a milestone piece of literature that provides clear direction for establishing a style of leadership that truly *expects* (and usually gets) performance that leads to outstanding results.

Bellman, Geoffrey M. *Getting Things Done When You Are Not in Charge: How to Succeed from a Support Position*. San Francisco: Berrett-Koehler, 1992.

Geoff Bellman addresses many of the frustrations that those of us who have been in support positions have experienced when trying to move our ideas through the corporate maze. We are not as powerless as we like to think we are. This book supports my concept of the *unit president*, showing practical ways of impacting organizational direction and results.

Block, Zenas, and MacMillan, Ian C. *Corporate Venturing: Create New Businesses in Your Firm.* Boston: Harvard Business School Press, 1993.

This book is designed for the internal champion, working under the corporate umbrella, who is charged with developing and marketing new ventures that are a distinct departure from the company's core products. Drawing on many real-world examples, it provides principles and techniques for making the new venture a success.

Collins, James C., and Porras, Jerry I. *Built to Last: Successful Habits of Visionary Companies.* New York: HarperCollins, 1994.

This book is a fascinating summary of research done with several companies the authors describe as *visionary* relative to several other successful but less-visionary companies in the same industries, all of which were founded before 1950. The "Twelve Shattered Myths" (such as "It takes a great idea to start a great company" and "Visionary companies require great and charismatic visionary leaders"), which are the theme of the book, provide eye-opening insights as well as methodologies for determining what makes the most sense for the future of your company.

Conner, Daryl R. *Management at the Speed of Change: How Resilient Managers Succeed and Prosper Where Others Fail.* New York: Villard Books, 1995.

Daryl Conner has been both a pioneer and a continual student in the field of change management. This book embodies the essence of his experience in working with a wide range of organizations as they move in dramatic new directions.

Drucker, Peter F. *Managing for the Future: The 1990s and Beyond.* New York: Truman Talley Books/Dutton, 1992.

Peter Drucker continues to be one of the world's most influential management thinkers, frequently years ahead of his time. This book presents a series of provocative and insightful essays under four broad headings: "Economics," "People," "Management," and "The Organization." "The Trend Toward Alliances for Progress" is a brief but precise set of guidelines for addressing one of the major business trends of the future.

Hammer, Michael, and Stanton, Steven E. *The Reengineering Revolution: A Handbook.* New York: HarperCollins, 1995.

This new book from the coauthor of *Reengineering the Corporation* addresses many of the successes and problems that have occurred within organizations that have undertaken reengineering efforts. It will be especially helpful to those managers who are seriously considering reengineering as a change methodology but who don't wish to get caught up in a "bandwagon" approach.

Leibfried, Kathleen H. J., and McNair, C. J. *Benchmarking: A Tool for Continuous Improvement*. New York: HarperCollins, 1992.
This book from The Coopers & Lybrand Performance Solutions Series is the most comprehensive publication on the subject that I have seen. It emphasizes the importance of using this approach as *a never-ending objective* in maintaining the competitive edge.

Naisbitt, John. *Global Paradox: The Bigger the World Economy, the More Powerful Its Smallest Players*. New York: Morrow, 1994.
John Naisbitt, of *Megatrends* fame, addresses the trend toward dramatic change in the ways that companies and countries do business. His premise is that "huge companies like IBM, Philips, and GM must break up to become confederations of small, autonomous, entrepreneurial companies if they are to survive." This is provocative reading from one of the foremost futurists of our time.

Osborne, David, and Gaebler, Ted. *Reinventing Government: How the Entrepreneurial Spirit Is Transforming the Public Sector*. Reading, Mass: Addison-Wesley, 1992.
This is not a government-bashing treatise. It is a rational approach to using modern management principles and techniques to address the unique management concerns of government operations. The book is amply illustrated with examples of governmental entities that are doing this successfully at the national, state, and local levels.

Schmidt, Warren H., and Finnegan, Jerome P. *TQManager: A Practical Guide for Managing in a Total Quality Organization*. San Francisco: Jossey-Bass, 1993.
Warren Schmidt and Jerry Finnegan have boiled down to the basics the concepts and competencies of the total-quality approach, without all the hoopla. If you want to learn how to make TQM work, this is the book to read.

Planning Theory and Practice

Allen, Louis A. *Making Managerial Planning More Effective*. New York: McGraw-Hill, 1982.

I had the privilege of working with Louis Allen in the mid 1960s while I was in a staff position at Rockwell International, to which he was serving as a consultant. He had a major impact on my managerial thinking and on my desire to become more involved in the planning process. This classic book provides comprehensive coverage of planning from the perspective of the individual manager rather than of the enterprise as a whole. Chapter Eight, "The Position Plan," is especially helpful for managers who need to define their own accountabilities as part of the total planning effort.

Austin, L. Allan, and Hall, Dean G. *COmpetitive REsourcing: How to Use Decision Packages to Make the Best Use of Human and Financial Assets*. New York: Amacom, 1989.

I have come to know Allan Austin as a brilliant strategic thinker with a strong international reputation. Few consultants in the field know how to address global competition as he does. This book is particularly directed toward managers in mature industries (those whose global market growth has dropped below 10 percent annually). Allan and his coauthor, Dean Hall, describe the COmpetitive REsourcing (CORE) process, which requires senior managers to identify their competitive gaps, establish strategies to reduce the gaps, and enlist the creativity and innovation needed from all levels of the organization to eliminate the gaps.

Below, Patrick J., Morrisey, George L., and Acomb, Betty L. *The Executive Guide to Strategic Planning*. San Francisco: Jossey-Bass, 1987.

This book helped establish the foundation from which the first two books in this series were derived. While I have made several modifications to the integrated planning process first introduced in *The Executive Guide*, the book still represents a sound approach to the strategic planning process.

Bryson, John M. *Strategic Planning for Public and Nonprofit Organizations: A Guide to Strengthening and Sustaining Organizational Achievement*. San Francisco: Jossey-Bass, 1988.

Recognizing that the principles and techniques of strategic planning are as important in the public and the nonprofit worlds as they are in corporate America, John Bryson shows how to make strategic planning work for city managers and administrators, cabinet secretaries, school superintendents and principals, sheriffs and police chiefs, elected and appointed officials of governments and public agencies, and boards of directors of nonprofit organizations.

de Bono, Edward. *de Bono's Thinking Course*, Rev. ed. United Kingdom: MICA Management Resources, 1994.

As de Bono says in the "Author's Note" in the book, "Thinking is the ultimate human resource. The quality of our future will depend entirely on the quality of our thinking. This applies on a personal level, a community level and on the world level." Since *strategic thinking* is a basic part of the planning process introduced in this series, I can think of no better source for learning the thinking process than one of the world's leading authorities on cognitive thinking.

Goodwin, B. Terence. *Write on the Wall: A How-To Guide for Effective Planning in Groups*. Alexandria, Va.: American Society for Training and Development (ASTD), 1994.

Since I am a strong proponent of the use of a skilled facilitator in the planning process, the title of this book caught my eye at a recent ASTD national conference. It is one of the most concise yet thorough guides to facilitation of the planning process that I have seen. I recommend it to anyone, brand new or experienced, who is charged with the responsibility of facilitating a group planning process.

Hamel, Gary, and Prahalad, C. K. *Competing for the Future: Breakthrough Strategies for Seizing Control of Your Industry and Creating the Markets of Tomorrow*. Boston: Harvard Business School Press, 1994.

One of the most insightful and provocative books to come out in recent years on preparing to make a difference in the marketplace of the future, this book is a wake-up call for managers who still believe that what has worked in the past will continue to produce the desired results in the future. One of the profound changes the authors see as necessary for those companies that expect to be successful in the future is the need to focus more on the development and enhancement of core competencies and less on gaining immediate market share. This is *must* reading for anyone who expects to compete successfully in the future.

Mintzberg, Henry. *The Rise and Fall of Strategic Planning*, New York: Free Press, 1994.

Although this appears to be an overt attack on strategic planning, it is more of a plea to do what is necessary to move an organization forward in meeting the challenges of the future. Mintzberg pulls no punches in assessing many of the accepted strategic planning theories and practices (if nothing else, it is entertaining reading in that respect). The final section of the book, "Planning, Plans, Planners," moves from the critical to the constructive, describing, among other factors, the new roles of planners as finders of strategy, as analysts, and as catalysts. His emphasis on coupling analysis and intuition helped clarify my thinking in drawing the distinctions among strategic thinking, long-range planning, and tactical planning.

Morrisey, George L. *Creating Your Future: Personal Strategic Planning for Professionals.* San Francisco: Berrett-Koehler, 1992.
This book shows how to apply the principles and techniques of strategic planning to your own career growth, personal life, business development, and financial planning.

Morrisey, George L. *Management by Objectives and Results in the Public Sector* and *Management by Objectives and Results for Business and Industry.* Reading, Mass.: Addison-Wesley, 1976, 1977.
These two books provide a how-to approach to making the MOR process work for managers in government and in business, respectively.

Morrisey, George L., Below, Patrick J., and Acomb, Betty L. *The Executive Guide to Operational Planning.* San Francisco: Jossey-Bass, 1987.
This book, together with my prior books on Management by Objectives and Results, provided a foundation for the third book in this series, *A Guide to Tactical Planning.*

Odiorne, George S. *Management by Objectives: A System of Managerial Leadership.* New York: Pitman, 1965.
George Odiorne was my colleague, mentor, and friend until his untimely passing a few years ago. This book was the one that put MBO on the map and helped make that concept one of the most enduring management "labels" of all time.

Odiorne, George S. *Strategic Management of Human Resources: A Portfolio Approach.* San Francisco: Jossey-Bass, 1984.
This book is especially helpful for those who are required to analyze human resources in the strategic planning process. George shows how to apply portfolio analysis to human resource management and offers practical approaches for managing and capitalizing on high-performing employees.

Porter, Michael E. *Competitive Strategy: Techniques for Analyzing Industries and Competitors* and *Competitive Advantage: Creating and Sustaining Superior Performance.* New York: Free Press, 1980, 1985.
These two landmark books provide a wealth of information on approaches and techniques for competitive analysis. They are especially useful for market analysts who are required to come up with the data needed to complete market segment analyses in highly competitive industries.

Ramsey, Jackson E., and Ramsey, Inez L. *Budgeting Basics: How to Survive the Budgeting Crisis.* New York: Franklin Watts, 1985.
In searching libraries, I found very few books that addressed budgeting in anything other than "accountingese." This one is clearly the exception. It takes a potentially dry subject and puts it into clear, easy-to-read, nonfinan-

cial terms. The authors use a continuing case study throughout that is fun to follow. The chapter "New Department Budgeting" is especially helpful; it provides a good start-to-finish method, including how to make estimates on workload, human resource skills, materials, and operating costs. The book provides everything a nonfinancial manager needs to know, and then some, about what goes into the preparation of budgets.

Redding, John C., and Catalanello, Ralph F. *Strategic Readiness: The Making of the Learning Organization*. San Francisco: Jossey-Bass, 1994.
This book expands on the concept of the learning organization introduced in Peter Senge's *The Fifth Discipline* (New York: Doubleday, 1990). Its main focus is not on individual learning or team learning but on the organization-wide process through which entire firms plan, implement, and modify strategic directions. It moves beyond abstract descriptions of learning organizations and offers numerous illustrations of learning organizations in action.

Ruskin, Arnold M., and Estes, W. Eugene. *What Every Engineer Should Know About Project Management* (2nd ed.). New York: Marcel Dekker, 1995.
Project management is a very precise form of tactical planning, one that is bread and butter for most engineers. Arnie Ruskin has been a friend and colleague for many years. He and coauthor Eugene Estes have written one of the most practical books I have seen on the subject. The chapters on "Control Techniques" and "Risk Management" are especially useful for engineers and managers whose very survival may depend on assessing and controlling costs.

Steiner, George A. *Strategic Planning: What Every Manager Must Know*. New York: Free Press, 1979.
George Steiner's contributions to strategic and long-range planning are legendary. This book provides a comprehensive approach to strategic planning, including a wide variety of analytical techniques. It is especially useful for those wanting an in-depth understanding of the strategic planning process.

Tomasko, Robert M. *Rethinking the Corporation: The Architecture of Change*. New York: Amacom, 1993.
This is a refreshing look at the process of moving an organization from where it is now to where it needs to be, using the logic of the architect. Tomasko's sense of direction for the new corporation is: "It will be a business with few walls. Its structure will minimize barriers between staff thinkers and line doers, between functions and divisions, and between the company and the outside world."

Treacy, Michael, and Wiersema, Fred. *The Discipline of Market Leaders: Choose Your Customers, Narrow Your Focus, Dominate Your Market*. Reading, Mass.: Addison-Wesley, 1995.

The word *focus* is one of the most important words in the planning lexicon. This book brings this message home with a vengeance. The authors have identified three distinct value disciplines: *operational excellence, product leadership,* and *customer intimacy.* Their position, backed by real-world examples, is that companies that are real market leaders select one of these disciplines on which to stake their market reputation, even though they may continue to address the remaining two disciplines. Understanding these three value disciplines and how they work can be a significant step in the formulation of corporate strategy.

Tregoe, Benjamin B., and Zimmerman, John W. *Top Management Strategy: What It Is and How to Make It Work.* New York: Simon & Schuster, 1980; and Tregoe, Benjamin B., Zimmerman, John W., Smith, Ronald A., and Tobia, Peter M. *Vision in Action: Putting a Winning Strategy to Work.* New York: Simon & Schuster, 1989.

The first of these two books introduced the concept of the *driving force* as a powerful tool for determining strategy or strategic direction. It significantly influenced my and my coauthors' interpretation of strategy in our book *The Executive Guide to Strategic Planning.* The second book describes how the Kepner-Tregoe team has expanded and applied their approach to strategy in several well-known organizations, including addressing the perceptions of several managers within those organizations.

Weiss, Alan. *Making It Work: Turning Strategy Into Action Throughout Your Organization.* New York: HarperCollins, 1990.

The focus in this book is on implementation. Alan's premise is that the failure of strategies is most often not the result of poorly conceived strategies but rather the result of poor implementation. In an entertaining manner, he suggests some solid techniques for translating strategic thinking and long-range planning into real-world action.

Index